REALTOR BRANDING:
Marketing Yourself for
REAL ESTATE SUCCESS

Irina Kim Sang

DEDICATION

A book is generally dedicated to someone special to the author: spouse, parents, children, and so forth. This book is dedicated to you – my fellow Realtors on a journey to success.

CONTENTS

ABOUT THIS BOOK

I wrote this book for the following reasons:

- When I started my real estate business three years ago, having a professional marketing background, I first researched all available resources, specifically books on the real estate subject. I was unable to locate a **single comprehensive, up-to-date source** dedicated to Realtor marketing and branding in order to launch my real estate business.

- Secondly, in search of specific instructions, I have attended more than sixty trainings, workshops, and seminars conducted by top industry professionals. I certainly collected good pieces of advice and plenty of motivation but still could not find a **comprehensive, structured marketing manual that applied specifically to real estate.**

- Finally, as a marketer, I recognized a missing link in the real estate business. Like many businesses, a Realtor's business tends to fail due to a lack of marketing fundamentals. Marketing plays a crucial role in the success of any venture, from marketing goods and services to launching political campaigns. In the real estate industry, everyone has a unique personality with a different educational background and professional experience. **Agents are primarily taught sales skills, which are based on a numbers game, but very few marketing skills, which are based on strategic approach.** The challenge is, how can you sell if you're unable to continually generate quality, targeted leads? Therefore, the Realtor's business is not only about sales but also and even more so about marketing yourself and your brand.

This book is unique in both content and structure, and I hope that you'll learn from it as I have in writing it. I wrote it in recognition of the **ever-growing need for marketing oneself and the unique challenges faced by Realtors in differentiating themselves and their brands in today's fast-paced, technology-driven, competitive environment.** Marketing knowledge and skills are needed more today than ever before.

This book is geared toward providing specific marketing knowledge and skills needed to launch or reposition your Realtor's business on a fast, direct track for success by saving you costly, time-consuming **trial and error**. Therefore, marketing becomes **your true investment rather than expense**.

This book is an excellent guide for:

- new agents who are just starting their careers;
- agents who have tried several things and got lost;
- seasoned agents who have been doing business successfully and are looking for a more structured and consolidated approach to their marketing and branding; and
- agents who have established «unpreferred» images in the market and

would like to rebrand and reposition themselves.

Since brands change over time, you need to be aware of the continual task of managing your brand and keeping it up-to-date. No brand will ever stay the same. This book will help you to stay on track and reinvent yourself for new opportunities.

I believe that one of the most vital marketing skills is an ability to systematize information. I've observed a great need for a visual framework – a blueprint or model – that real estate professionals can use as a marketing foundation to build successful businesses. To satisfy this need is the main purpose of this book.

This book details my **7 Ps PERSONAL BRANDING MODEL.** This model not only gives you a systematic approach but also opens up all key components and their relationship at every developmental stage of building your real estate brand.

- *P1 - Chapter 1 - PRODUCT: Knowing Yourself.* The beginning of the branding process is a detailed product assessment; in this case the product is *You.* You need to take time and be honest with yourself about your potential.
- *P2 - Chapter 2 - PEOPLE AND PLACE: Knowing Your Niche.* Are you interacting with and trying to promote yourself to the right people? This chapter helps you to categorize all potential **customer profiles and target audiences** to communicate your brand.
- *P3 - Chapter 3 - POSITIONING: Aligning Yourself with Your Niche.* What is your value proposition? What differentiates you from your competition? All the information collected in chapters 1 and 2 prepares you to be able to develop your personal profile and your unique promise of value, your **Unique Selling Proposition (USP).** If you don't have it, potential customers don't have any reasons to choose you. You blend in with the other thousands of licensed real estate agents.
- *P4 - Chapter 4 - PACKAGING: Designing Brand Identity.* Package yourself, from your personal story to all **visual components** of your brand.
- *P5 - Chapter 5 - PROMOTION: Communicating Your Brand Online and Offline.* Brand your traditional real estate communication tools. Brand your online and offline **Integrated Marketing Communication (IMC).** Your goal is to express your personal brand in all marketing materials, self-expressions, and best expressions. Create a communication plan, formed by marketing campaigns and your unique series of messages. You need a communication plan so that you're sharing your brand on your own terms – not leaving anything to chance.
- *P6 - Chapter 6 - PLATFORMS: Building and Nurturing Your Relationship Network.* Real estate is a «People Business,» and **building long-term, loyal relationships** is the key to a real estate success.

- *P7 – Chapter 7 – PROJECTION: Pursuing the Future with Persistence.* Personal Branding isn't a one-time project. It's an ongoing endeavor that has to be **managed over time.**

If you realize the importance of Personal Branding, this book will serve you as a blueprint to develop and maintain your unique trademark – *You*. It's your continual reference, based on the needs you'll have on your real estate journey.

This book is based on the technology of today and will be updated on a regular basis with the latest sources and advice.

This book is your marketing investment in you, toward your real estate success.

In order to maximize the value of this book, it's advisable to do the exercises as illustrated.

 Apply to Your Brand

 Review Detailed List

 Review Flowchart

ENJOY PERSONAL BRANDING: A JOURNEY TO DISCOVERING YOU!

INTRODUCTION

The Power of Personal Branding in Real Estate

So what exactly is Personal Branding? Your personal brand is your reputation, as defined by your character. Your personal brand is also your legacy; it's the way others remember you – through your actions, your expertise, and the emotional connections you make. Your personal brand shows your authenticity from inside out.

You already have a personal brand, whether you know it or not. Think for a minute what people would say about you if you're not present in the room: «She is so creative» or «I can trust him as I would trust myself».

Personal Branding is about expressing your authentic self by allowing you to be the person you're meant to be. However, it's not just a fill-in-the-blank exercise. It's a strategic process. Only through Personal Branding you can discover how to identify and communicate your unique promise of value, your Unique Selling Proposition (USP).

Your personal brand acts as a filter that helps you make decisions relevant to who you are and what you stand for. It identifies what makes you unique and clearly communicates your individuality to the people who need to know about you.

You as Your Own Chief Marketing Officer

People need just three things to be sold on you as their Agent of Choice. They need to like you, believe in you, and trust you. Staying authentic and being relevant create an honest, assuring, and unforgettable exposure and a memorable experience. Being slick, programmed, and focused on the deal rather than the client may get you one sale, but it won't create a lasting or enjoyable career.

Why should you care? First, because in a noisy and cluttered world, the need for individuality has never been greater. Also, because the real estate profession is a people business, people remember great people through emotions as a result of interactions. In fact, according to services marketing research, clients will typically only remember either extremely positive encounters- when they were delighted, surprised, amazed, or inspired – or extremely negative encounters, when they were shocked by the service provider's unattractive behavior. In other words, people don't remember situations that are adequate in nature, in which their expectations matched perceptions. Now, think about how much room we – real estate professionals have to delight our clients and the refore be remembered and buzzed about, resulting in free, positive word-of-mouth promotion and referral business.

Second, if you don't take the time to define, design, and manage your personal brand, someone else will do it for you by default. These are just fundamentals of Public Relations. Do a quick test: think how people would speak about you if you were to step out of the room. What reputation and image would they describe?

Finally, you need to control your brand, because you're remarkable and special. The process of creating a personal brand is about taking charge of your reputation, which will allow you to project to the world what is special about you. Don't let people make a blind guess! Discover who you are – your passion – package it, and consistently communicate the value of the *Special You.*

This is the basis for success today. You have to stand out from the rest of the bunch – on your terms, in your unique way.

You don't have to be famous to benefit from Personal Branding. The goals behind it are to expand exposure, increase your value, and create a *Bigger You* – in order to realize your full potential.

Since the moment when globalization and social media wiped out all possible geographic borders and time zones, Personal Branding has become far more relevant than ever before. The good news is that the world has become smaller and more connected. The bad news is that it has become more competitive at the individual level. Differentiation and focusing on more defined customer niches are now a business priority. Even though word-of-mouth advertising and referrals still play an important role in the real estate business, your presence on the web and clear positioning will allow you to cut through the noise and create «followship». If branding is approached strategically, there is tremendous opportunity to create landmarks in the branding landscape.

Personal Branding isn't rocket science. Creating the image that defines your unique value is a combination of pragmatic thinking and the art of creativity, both online and offline, which anyone can master. You want to avoid having no image, an unclear image, a weak and meaningless image, or a «me too» image. If you don't care about your personal brand, why would customers care?

In the corporate world, there are separate marketing structures and functions in charge of brand development and brand management. But in real estate, you're all in one – you're it. You have to wear the Chief Marketing Officer's hat, the Brand Manager's hat, the Creative Director's hat, and the Advertising Agency's hat. By learning several tools, techniques, principles, and processes you can develop a strong brand. This is a great part of the business that you can master, because at the end of the day, you're the one whose reputation is in the spotlight.

I want to help you feel confident in pursuing the creative analytics of branding yourself. Learn the skills that will pay off regardless of what opportunity you go after. And always remember, strong brands stay consistent but never the same – they evolve as they grow and as the market environment changes.

Although Personal Branding is not rocket science, it is not an easy task as filling in the blanks. If you truly want to differentiate and be remembered as the number-one source when the client has a need, you'll have to be aware of the changing environment (the market, trends, and opportunities). Think critically about how your assets can be transitioned to match new opportunities if needed. Your personal brand, without any doubt, is your most important intangible asset. Invest in it, and you'll be rewarded.

Whether you're aware of it or not, whether you like it or not, you already have some form of personal brand, because your personal brand is your image and reputation by others. Society perceives you in a certain way and puts you in a certain category. A combination of your personality, gestures, body language, behaviors, style of dressing, responses, and reactions create a perception of *You*.

But more importantly, your knowledge, skills, and values, in most cases, are hidden, and these most important parts of your brand will stay covered unless you take advantage of packaging them and communicating them through the message you give to your target audience. People aren't mind readers; they can't discover how good you are on their own. You have to show it to them by developing branding strategy and tactics.

Try to answer the following question: Are you known for something of value? Or are you a victim of others branding you?

An Average versus a Successful Agent Profile

Ask yourself the following: What is the profile of my ideal client? What type of clientele and real estate would I like to focus on? Try to define it. You want to identify what you love doing and do it with passion. Real estate isn't a job; it's your own business. Therefore, you better define who you want to work with.

It's like taking a private elevator versus a public one. A public elevator is likely to stop on every floor, meaning you're dealing with every client type and wasting time in the long run, while the private elevator is the direct and only access to your floor, meaning you're dealing with the customers you have a passion to work with.

Your personal brand can be as powerful as Starbucks or Nike among your potential clients. Developing a powerful brand is a process that considers the needs of customers, the value of an offering – your product – and the message that will entice customers. Branding is all about differentiation, about not being just another real estate agent. In order to establish how your brand is different, you – as the Chief Marketing Officer (CMO) of your own corporation – must first get to know your value offering and the customers you would like to service. You must know them inside out. Discovering what makes you unique is the key.

Entertainers, athletes, and political candidates, for example, create personal brands. These unique personal brands not only result in greater sales and stronger reputations but also attract the right types of clients, employees, investors, and advertisers.

The real estate industry offers a variety of business opportunities. Choosing what you would like to focus on starts with determining what you enjoy the most, pursuing that area of the field, and balancing it with the economic returns. This will become your initial strategy. It doesn't necessarily mean that you'll always stick to the same strategy. You'll need to adjust it as time goes on, because nothing is constant in the real estate business. External opportunities will always change, and your objective as CMO is to continually oversee the market and forecast opportunities to take advantage of them.

Fundamentally, a brand is a unique identity and a coherent message that sets *You* and *Your Services* apart from the competition. We usually associate a brand with its logo and slogan. In fact, some brands are so powerful that advertisements need few words to describe those products and services; we immediately form associations in our mind. Figuring out your brand identity is a challenging task. You're a complex human being with many talents, interests, skills, and viewpoints. Discovering which ones you want to package and which ones are important among your potential clients – your employers – are the major benefits of the process of designing and managing your own personal brand.

In order to develop a brand, study the product to find out what the product can do. Then identify key performance characteristics and product features that can differentiate that offering, and determine whether these differences are meaningful to a potential client. Then find a way to package the offering and communicate its differences in a way that offers the client a clear understanding of why he or she should choose your product over others and what benefits it will bring him or her.

For the client, it's always a trade-off between the *Value* he or she receives and the *Perceived Cost* he or she has to give in exchange. In Personal Branding, the first question to ask is what your *Features* are. Why would an employer want your skills? What problems can you solve? What results will your skills achieve?

When your brand is clear to you, just like a marketing expert, you will know what to communicate to your customer. Because you will have discovered your customer's needs, you'll have the confidence that your messages–whether delivered via direct mail, closing gifts, prelisting packages, listing presentations, complimentary Comparative Market Analysis (CMA)s, or listing presentations – will hit the mark. The bottom line is that you want to be hired every day, several times a day!

Benefits of Your Own Personal Branding

- A strong identity that you continually communicate to advance your real estate career.
- A focus on your customers' (potential employers') needs.
- An understanding of the benefits of your skills, knowledge, and experience and certainly an understanding of your weaknesses and areas for personal development.
- A development of strategies to reach targeted employers.
- A new attitude that puts you in charge of your career so that it's able to adapt to change and you can maintain lifetime employability.

The reason most people never reach their goals is that they don't define them or ever seriously consider them as believable or achievable.

«Winners can tell you where they are going, what they plan to do along the way, and who will be sharing the adventure with them.»

– Denis Waitley

You're on your own. Take charge of your personal brand.

7 Ps PERSONAL BRANDING MODEL

CHAPTER 1

PRODUCT

Knowing Yourself

REALTOR BRANDING:
Marketing Yourself for **REAL ESTATE SUCCESS**

PRODUCT
Knowing
Yourself

> Defining who you are today and who you want to be tomorrow is the foundation of **Branding**. Without this discovery, you're merely marketing something or shooting without a target.

Personal Branding is all about authenticity, and you need to define yourself before you can market yourself authentically.

The first P of the Branding Model – **PRODUCT** – is your critical homework. Take the time to think about each piece of information that you need to gather about yourself. Enjoy the self-assessment process and discover your uniqueness.

Figure 1-1 summarizes five steps that will take you through the process of self-assessment.

Figure 1-1:
Chapter 1 Summary

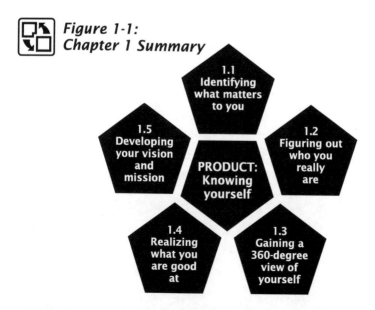

1.1. Identifying What Matters to You

Identifying what mattes to you sounds like an easy task. However, most people don't give it special thought. Completing exercises in this section of the book will assist you in becoming more aware of yourself, your choices, and your behaviors.

1.1.1. Knowing Your Needs

The process of answering the question «What matters to me?» starts with identifying what you need. Needs are important to consider because people commonly stop themselves from trying new things or taking risks for fear of putting their basic needs in jeopardy.

> *Needs direct your feelings and influence your values and your motivation.*

According to Abraham Maslow's well-known theory, Maslow's Hierarchy of Needs, there are five levels of needs. Starting at the bottom, each level of need must be met in order for someone to be able to consider and work toward meeting the next level of needs. These are the levels:

- **Physiological** (food, shelter, sleep, water, oxygen, sex, freedom of movement, moderate temperature)
- **Safety** (security, stability, safety of body and family, freedom from violence, rituals and routines)
- **Belonging and Love** (friendships, family, sexual intimacy, community)
- **Esteem** (self-confidence, mutual respect of and for others, achievement, recognition)
- **Self-actualization** (knowledge, understanding, peace, self-fulfillment, life mission, pursuit of inner talents, creativity, beauty)

Figure 1-2:
Maslow's Hierarchy of Needs

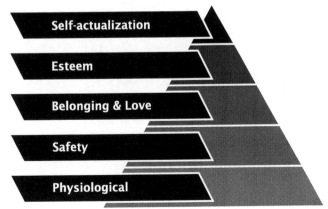

The following two examples illustrate application of the theory to the real estate career using two polar levels of needs:

- **Real Estate Career Physiological Needs**: A regular paycheck, scheduled breaks, and predictable work hours. This set of conditions will satisfy your physiological needs if you're an office or administrative assistant, data entry specialist, or closing coordinator.

- **Real Estate Career Self-Actualization Needs**: Being able to fully use your talents at work, contributing to the professional development of others, knowing your purpose in life, having bigger dreams, meeting challenges, and having a sense of mastery.

In the table below, try to indicate what your needs are at the moment. Which of them have been met? Which of them have not?

Figure 1-3:
Needs Assessment

Question	Fill in Your Answer
What needs of yours are met?	
What needs of yours aren't met?	

1.1.2. Focusing on Things You Love to Do

Your interests or passions are things that intrigue you and motivate you to devote energy to them. They determine how you want to spend your time.

> *Your interests (likes/dislikes, talents, passions) often develop early in life, but not every interest is supported by a talent or ability, so your level of engagement may depend on your level of skill.*

Figure 1-4 summarizes a range of tasks and activities you engage in during the course of business.

Figure 1-4:
Interest Inventory

(Susan Chritton, *Personal Branding for Dummies*, Hoboken: John Wiley and Sons, Inc. [2014], #61.)

Interest	Description
Researching	Research, observe, investigate, study, perceive, sense, measure, test, inspect, examine
Analyzing	Analyze, compare, extract, correlate, derive, evaluate, differentiate, identify
Interpreting	Interpret, explain, understand, portray, advise
Problem solving	Solve, troubleshoot, improve, critique, redirect, redesign, restructure
Systematizing	Systematize, coordinate, organize, develop procedures
Planning	Plan short-term, plan long-term, forecast, strategize, set goals
Managing	Manage, supervise, control, direct, budget, administer, delegate
Leading	Lead, govern, inspire, motivate, assert, decide, advise
Decision making	Decide, judge, select, decide under pressure, arbitrate
Following through	Persist, persevere, show tenacity, tie up all loose ends, bring to closure
Mentoring	Mentor, teach, coach, counsel constructively, help others to grow professionally and personally
Innovating	Innovate, invent, change, develop, devise, break with convention
Imagining	Imagine, visualize, conceptualize, fantasize
Visioning	Envision the future clearly, ask «What if?» and «Why not?» and act to find the answers

Synthesizing	Synthesize, adapt, bring together with imagination
Creating	Create, draw, sketch, sculpt, perform with originality
Counseling	Empathize, understand needs/feelings of others, relate to issues and concerns of others, comfort, offer kindness, help others, be friendly and attentive
Listening	Listen actively and understand the messages others are delivering
Communicating in Writing	Write clearly, concisely, and effectively, spot grammatical errors, use editorial ability
Communicating Verbally	Speak clearly, concisely, and effectively; use the spoken word to get results
Persuading Verbally	Persuade, convince, influence, overcome opposition, sell
Negotiating	Mediate, negotiate, intervene, resolve differences, arbitrate
Initiating	Take the initiative, be among the first to do or try, get things started
Changing Dynamics	Be flexible, adapt easily to change, be aware, go with the flow
Working on a Team	Work well with a team, be a team player
Assembling	Assemble, build, prepare, fabricate, rebuild, fashion
Installing	Install, fit, tailor, customize, test
Operating	Operate, run, maintain, fix, set up

Use Figure 1-4 to help you answer questions in Figure 1-5, which will allow you to discover and/or determine your inclinations.

Figure 1-5:
Your Likes and Dislikes

Question	Fill in Your Answer
What current and past activities do you like most? (Think back even to your school days.)	
In your current line of work, what activities do you not like?	
What kinds of volunteer work do you enjoy doing?	
What hobbies do you spend the most time on?	

1.1.3. Getting to Know the Authentic You

> *The Personal Branding process helps you own who you are so that you don't waste your life wishing to be someone else.*

In this process you need to take a realistic look at yourself to understand all the factors that make you who you are. The goal is to live and thrive as an authentic human being, and it's absolutely worth the effort.

1.1.4. Considering Your Life Circumstances

Whether you're just joining the Realtor community or have been building your real estate legacy, Personal Branding Principles help to shape and allow you to enjoy your career journey at any stage of your professional development.

> *The beauty of a personal brand is that it's not static. Your personal brand will evolve as you become more experienced and as market environment changes.*

Throughout your lifetime, certain things about your personality will change, and you'll gain more expertise.

1.1.5. Defining Your Meaning for Success

Embarking on the path of Personal Branding forces you to question what success looks like for you on a personal level. Does success mean what others see in you? Are your achievements the measure of your success? How motivated are you by your internal self-actualization needs?

> *Follow your heart. Identify your mission in life. Identify your strengths, values, passions, and goals. Invest in yourself. Know what you don't know, and get help with what you need to move forward. Trust your outrageous ideas.*

You may not know what success means to you as you begin this journey, but chances are you'll have a much clearer idea after you've worked through this Personal Branding Model.

1.2. Figuring Out Who You Really Are

> «Today you are you, that is truer than true. There is no one alive who is youer than you.»
>
> – Dr. Seuss

The essential step in developing your personal brand is knowing yourself. In this process, you need to answer questions to discover your authenticity and understand what you need in order to live your mission through your personal brand.

Taking an honest assessment about who you are and what you want means looking at what you do well and recognizing limitations. You definitely should seek input from others during this process. However, you can't let them determine who you'll be.

> *Personal Branding is about you being you in the most authentic way.*

And if you truly want to succeed and shine, you have to figure out how to differentiate yourself from the crowd. Getting to know yourself is truly the toughest part of crafting your Personal Brand.

1.2.1. Shaping Your Identity

Branding guru Robin Fisher Roffer believes that Personal Branding helps you to «know who you are and be valued for it, to attract what you want, to become more attractive to others, to inspire confidence, to walk your path with integrity, and to distinguish yourself in whatever field you've chosen.»

As you embark on the Personal Branding journey, the starting point is self-recognition, knowing who you are. You need to be able to look closely at yourself, be able to listen to what others think about you, and be willing to grow and change.

Through this process you'll discover your uniqueness and how to leverage it in the marketplace. As you get clarity about your vision, values, passion, purpose, and goals, you'll be able to demonstrate your authenticity with confidence and certainty, rather than trying to practice chameleon life by changing colors. This clarity helps you live more consistently, which is vital to living a successful life.

1.2.2. Defining Your Values

Values are the emotional currency of your life.

Values are the core principles and drivers that give meaning to your life. They're defined as a set of standards that determine your attitudes, choices, and actions. Although you're changing, your core values typically remain the same.

Values help you establish your sense of purpose and direction. They act as guideposts that assist you in evaluating choices in your life. They are the guiding principles by which you lead and live your life. When you're establishing a personal brand, you must understand your core values because they are the heart of who you are.

In Figure 1-6, choose top five values that characterize you the most and place them in the priority list in Figure 1-7. Then think about the real estate industry. How well do you think your chosen values will be satisfied in your real estate profession? Rate them on a scale of high, medium, and low.

Figure 1-6:
Values
(Kim Richmond, *Brand You*, Upper Saddle River: Prentice Hall [2009]: #12.)

Value	Description
Achievement	To accomplish important things
Advancement	To reach the top in an organization or profession
Adventure	To take risks, to discover new things
Autonomy	To set your own schedule and priorities
Balance	To be able to balance your work life with your other interests
Challenge	To be involved in interesting work, to solve a variety of problems
Community	To be a part of a group, to support community activities
Contribution	To contribute to society, to have an impact on people's lives
Creativity	To be original, to express yourself
Expertise	To be respected for your competence, to be known as an expert in your field
Friendship	To develop friendships at work, to have time for friends
Fun	To have fun, to enjoy your life and work
Growth	To develop personally and professionally
Health/Wellness	To be physically and emotionally healthy
Helpful	To be of service to others, to contribute to the well-being of others
High Income	To be financially successful

Influence	To have influence over decisions, to influence people through your work
Integrity	To stand up for your beliefs, to be honest
Leadership	To motivate others to achieve goals
Passion	To care deeply about your work, commitment to a cause
Recognition	To earn respect and recognition from others
Security	To achieve stable work and financial situation
Self-expression	To be able to act in a way consistent with your values and beliefs, to be able to express your ideas
Spirituality	To be at peace with yourself, to achieve inner harmony
Structure	To have order and a predictable work environment
Teamwork	To accomplish goals as a member of a team
Trust	To work in an environment in which people trust one another
Work independently	To be responsible for your own accomplishments

Figure 1-7:
Your Top Five Values

Value	High	Medium	Low
1.			
2.			

3.			
4.			
5.			

When marketers design products, they look at them on different Product Levels in order to have a clear understanding of how they will meet customers' needs, challenge competition, and wow clients. These are the five Product Levels:

- **Core Level**
- **Basic Level**
- **Expected Level**
- **Augmented Level**
- **Potential Level**

For your Personal Branding purposes, I've interpreted this basic marketing approach into the analogy of **Onion Layers**, the layers of your Personal Brand (Figure 1-8).

 Figure 1-8:
The Personal Brand Onion Layers

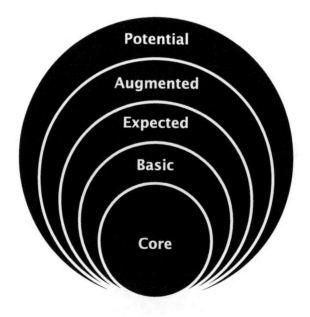

Personal Brand starts with the **Core Layer** – the **Values**, which you have already discovered and listed in Figure 1-7, followed by the rest of your personal characteristics, which you will discover about yourself in this chapter.

> *Your top values are the driving force of your behavior throughout your life. Unless a major, life-changing event happens, in general, personal values stay consistent.*

The **Basic Layer** encompasses your interests, talents, and passions, which you discovered in Figures 1-4 and 1-5.

The **Expected Layer** encompasses all of your formal skills and knowledge, such as educational degrees, certificates, and other skills you have sufficient experience in. When you start your real estate career, this layer may look totally irrelevant. Your task is to find the relationship among your existing set of skills and translate them into the **List of Strengths** necessary for your real estate business. For example, if your career background is nursing, customer-care skills could be at the top of your *Strengths* List. Or if you're a former car salesman, you're most likely to have strong sales skills.

The **Augmented Layer** represents the emotional side of your brand – your personality, authenticity, and personal style – which are usually the greatest differentiators of brands, especially among people in the business of real estate. Customers typically base their decision making on rational behavior when purchasing products; however, in real estate, it's not uncommon to choose a Realtor simply because «he is a great guy»,which is pure emotional decision making.

The final **Potential Layer** demonstrates an area where your brand could grow, evolve, improve, and add credibility, depending on market conditions, opportunities, challenges, and competition.

In Figure 1-9 summarize your own Personal Brand «Onion Layers».

Figure 1-9:
Your Personal Brand Onion Layers

Layer	Fill in Your Answer
Core Layer (Values)	

Basic Layer (Your interests, talents, and passions)	
Expected Layers (Skills, knowledge, formal education)	
Augmented Layer (Personal style)	
Potential Layers (Areas to grow your personal brand; additional qualifications, expertise, and designations)	

1.3. Gaining a 360-Degree View of Yourself

Any time you seriously want to do some branding work, you need to know the opinions of others. Most people naturally would prefer not to know what others really think about them, but in order to build a real brand you need to collect data from a broader base than just your own personal opinion about yourself. The two images might be pretty different. The sooner you know about those differences, the more efficient you branding process will be.

In the corporate world, in order to discover those differences, an individual often uses what is called a 360-Degree Assessment. The idea behind this technique is that you gather opinions about your behavior and performance of all aspects of your job by all parties you interact with, such as your boss, coworkers, subordinates, administrative staff, suppliers, clients, and public.

1.3.1. The 360-Degree Reach Assessment

The most relevant way to approach the 360-Degree Assessment in the Personal Branding process is the **360 Reach Tool** that was designed by Reach Personal Branding. It's the leading Personal Branding assessment that helps you understand your brand from the outside in. This tool will help you answer the question «Who are You?» It helps you look at your character and pull out the information at the heart of your brand. It helps you to understand your reputation and insights as perceived by others.

There is a free version that you can use to gather your raw data, but a full version provides a great, very user-friendly report.

Visit www.reachcc.com/reach/survey/nsf to access this tool.

1.3.2. Conducting Self-Analysis

The goal here is for you to look at yourself objectively and give a fair evaluation of your strengths, weaknesses, and attributes. In order to discover yourself, go through this process in a fun way with an open mind and attitude.

1.3.3. Researching Insights from Friends and Family

The way the online assessment tool works is that you supply names and e-mail addresses of your friends and family who you deem know you well, and the company running the assessment reaches out to those people on your behalf, similar to a background-check interview. The best outcome results from reaching out to those people who know you well enough to answer questions about your top strengths or attributes. Ideally you need fifteen to thirty respondents. (Make sure that your chosen respondents are aware of the survey and are willing to participate; otherwise, you'll need to reach out to twice as many people, as the usual response rate is only about 40-50 percent.) When you e-mail your friends and family regarding the upcoming research, encourage them to provide honest and detailed feedback and mention that you appreciate their time and honest opinions. The responses are kept anonymous.

1.3.4. Reacting to Feedback

I believe one of the biggest surprises when receiving the results of the 360 Reach Assessment is the possible discrepancy between the two images: what you think of yourself and what others' perceptions of you are. This research tool has a comparison column where you'll find top attributes you've listed of yourself next to what others see in you.

The question to be asked is, do you want to be seen more as you see yourself or as those who know you best see you? The obvious goal is to close the gap between the two perceptions, your own and others'.

1.4. Realizing What You're Good At

The next step in developing your Personal Brand is conducting **SWOT Analysis** (Figure 1-10), a process of discovering and evaluating

- **internal factors (Strengths and Weaknesses)** and
- **external factors (Opportunities and Threats).**

Figure 1-10:
SWOT Analysis

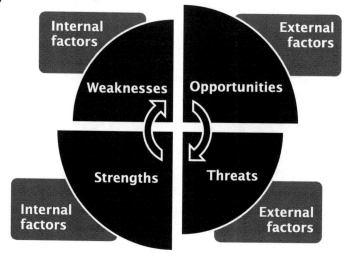

In this part of the branding process, you'll be able to advance your self-discovery by focusing on your strengths.

Figure 1-11 summarizes eight categories of skills. In order to evaluate your skill set, use Figure 1-12 to rate your level of enjoyment and degree of mastering these skills.

Figure 1-11:
Eight Categories of Skills

Interpret the results of this exercise in relationship with the skills top Realtors should have. Summarize your strengths and weaknesses.

Figure 1-12:
Skills Inventory (Expanded and Based on Figure 1-4:
Interest Inventory)

Skill	Enjoyment (1–5)	Degree of Skill (1–5)
COMMUNICATION SKILLS		
Persuading verbally: persuade, convince, influence, overcome opposition, sell		
Resolving conflicts, building consensus		
Communicating verbally: speak clearly, concisely, and effectively; use the spoken word to get results		
Giving effective presentations		
Developing compelling sales approaches		
Listening: listen actively and understand the message others are delivering		
Communicating in writing: write clearly, concisely, and effectively; spot grammatical errors; use editorial ability		
Counseling: empathize, understand needs/feelings of others, relate to issues and concerns of others, comfort, offer kindness, help others, be friendly and attentive		
Mentoring: mentor, teach, coach, give advice, counsel constructively, help others to grow professionally and personally		

Working on a team: work well with a team, be a team player, collaborate		
Instructing, training people to perform new tasks		
Interpreting/Explaining: interpret, explain, understand, portray, advise, explain complex ideas in everyday language		
Negotiating: mediate, negotiate, intervene, resolve differences, arbitrate		

USING INFORMATION SKILLS

Researching: research, observe, investigate, study, perceive, sense, measure, test, inspect, examine		
Systematizing: systematize, coordinate, organize, classify information, devise classification systems, develop procedures		
Analyzing: analyze, compare, extract, correlate, derive, evaluate, differentiate, identify		
Problem solving: solve, troubleshoot, improve, critique, redirect, redesign, restructure		
Creating useful reports		

MANAGING/LEADING SKILLS

Managing: manage, supervise, control, direct, budget, administer, delegate, coordinate, and organize work teams		

Leading: lead, govern, inspire and motivate others to achieve goals, assert, decide, advise, mentor, build trust		
Visioning: envision the future clearly, ask «What if?» and «Why not?» and act to find the answers		
Managing multiple projects		
Initiating: take the initiative, be among the first to do or try, get things started, initiate and execute a plan, task, or idea		
Initiating change: be flexible, adapt easily to change, be aware, go with the flow		
Coaching, developing others		
Decision making: decide, judge, select, decide under pressure, arbitrate		
Following through: persist, persevere, show tenacity, tie up all loose ends, bring to closure		

PLANNING SKILLS

Planning: plan short-term, plan long-term, forecast, strategize, set goals		
Creating effective solutions to problems		
Estimating, reviewing project schedules		

Preparing budgets, computing and justifying costs		
Establishing cost controls		

CREATIVITY SKILLS

Creating: create, draw, sketch, sculpt, perform with originality		
Innovating: innovate, invent, change, develop, devise, break with convention		
Imagining: imagine, visualize, conceptualize, fantasize		
Synthesizing: synthesize, adapt, bring together with imagination		

CUSTOMER SERVICE SKILLS

Focusing on customer needs		
Building and maintaining relationships		

BUSINESS DEVELOPMENT SKILLS

Generating income		
Identifying and capitalizing on opportunities		

OPERATIONS SKILLS		
Installing: install, fit, tailor, customize, test		
Operating: operate, run, maintain, fix, set up		

Now, in Figure 1-13, list your seven strongest skills, chosen from Figure 1-12. Note that these skills will most likely be the ones you're enjoying the most and have mastered.

Figure 1-13:
Your Top Skills

Skill	Enjoyment (1–5)	Degree of Skill (1–5)
1.		
2.		
3.		
4.		
5.		
6.		
7.		

1.4.1. Capitalizing on Your Strengths

Instead of wasting energy on redeeming your weaknesses, focus on capitalizing your strengths. After discovering the best of you through self-assessment, the next step is to analyze which of your personal qualities will be the most appealing to your target niche.

When you're able to draw this conclusion, you'll be able to proceed to the «packaging» stage by designing the message and choosing the channel to reach your target niche. You'll discover in chapter 4 how to «package» your brand.

1.4.2. Neutralizing Your Weaknesses

We all have weaknesses; however, I believe that the strengths we possess are much more powerful and overshadow any weakness we might have. My suggestion is to deal with weaknesses through
* planning and time management
* delegation
* outsourcing
* teaming up or partnering on a task
* additional training

1.4.3. Spotting Your Uniqueness

Each individual is unique in nature, and this is great news. Acknowledging your unique characteristics makes you human. This connection to your humanness is what authenticity is all about. In other words, let your personality shine.

1.4.4. Internal Factors – S and W of the SWOT Analysis

Let's now summarize your internal factors: strengths and weaknesses. Earlier in the chapter, we addressed Product Levels using the analogy of the Onion Layers as the levels on which you can build your brand. You can't simply say, «I'm good at everything,» or «Call me for all your real estate needs.» You need to choose your major selling feature and carry it through consistently in all your actions. In other words, when people around you can name one quality that you want to be associated with, it means that you're able to consistently communicate that message and establish your reputation based on it.

At this point you've reached the end of the self-evaluation process. Summarize all your findings in Figure 1-14.

Figure 1-14:
SWOT Analysis Part I: Strengths and Weaknesses

SWOT Factor	Your Strengths	Your Action
S = Strengths	*Fill in Your Answer*	
What do you do well? What do others see as your strengths? What unique resources do you have available? • Values • Skills • Passions • Hobbies • Interests • Formal education • Work experience		Capitalize on your strengths
	Your Weaknesses	**Your Action**
W = Weaknesses	*Fill in Your Answer*	
What can you improve? What holds you back? What do others see as your weaknesses?		Neutralize your weaknesses

1.5. Developing Your Vision and Mission

1.5.1. The Vision Statement

A vision statement is based on personal values and beliefs and captures your ultimate purpose or calling in life. It involves you envisioning your future and capturing a big picture of what you stand for and what you see happening for yourself. It's an overreaching, broad-based picture of who you are envisioning yourself to be and what you have to offer the world. It doesn't address the «how» behind your vision. The «how» is the aim of your mission statement. Both your vision and your mission statements are dynamic – not static. Over time they may develop and evolve.

> A personal vision statement or personal philosophy is what you feel you would like to become in life. There are no right or wrong answers. Defining your vision statement is just a way to put your purpose or calling into words.

Here are some questions to ask yourself to help you formulate your vision:

Figure 1-15:
Vision Questions

Question	Fill in Your Answer
When you think of the best version of yourself, what are you doing for work?	
What would you do if you were not afraid to fail?	
What would you be doing if you could do exactly what you wanted to?	

Figure 1-16:
Write Your Vision Statement

Vision Statement

1.5.2. The Mission Statement

A mission statement follows from the vision statement by outlining the process behind which the vision will be achieved. It points toward the «how-to», the execution and functions by which your vision will be lived. It's more detail oriented than the vision statement as well as more concrete and tangible. It reminds you of whether you are on track or off track with the goals you've set.

A corporation starts its strategic plans with a mission statement. The mission defines an overall purpose and what the business hopes to achieve in terms of its customers, products, and resources.

> *Your personal mission statement defines your daily journey with your vision in mind.*

Your mission should focus on your work and not on a generic goal such as «to find a balance between work and family». It should be narrow enough to give you a sense of focus but broad enough to adapt to future opportunities.

To develop your mission statement, think about these questions:
- What is important to you?
- Who you are?
- What do you stand for?
- What do you like to do?
- Why do you want to do it?

When writing your mission statement,
- make it memorable;
- focus on a single theme (don't try to be all things to all people);
- make it clear and concise;
- make sure it energizes you and rallies you to action;
- let it serve to guide you as you make decisions;
- think of nouns that describe you;
- add verbs defining what you want to do in the world; and
- add your picture of what a perfect world would look like.

Treat your mission statement as your personal mantra. Like a corporation, don't hide your mission statement; instead, find a way to display it. It will help you stay focused on your goals and guide your decisions.

Figuring out your mission sounds simple, but it's often hard. Typically, the greater the mission, the more simply it can be stated. Your mission needs to include your enthusiasm for life. If you have no passion for your mission, then it's not really your mission.

A strong mission is clear and powerful, and it encourages you to want to accomplish your vision. A well-written mission statement helps you consciously create and move forward from what currently is to what could be.

Figure 1-17:
Write Your Mission Statement

Mission Statement

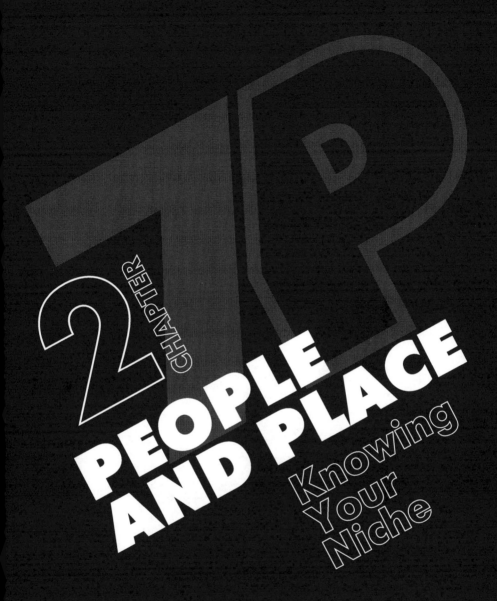

CHAPTER 2

PEOPLE AND PLACE

Knowing Your Niche

2 PEOPLE AND PLACE
Knowing Your Niche

The second P of the Branding Model – **PEOPLE AND PLACE** – focuses on identification of your target customers.

Figure 2-1:
Chapter 2 Summary

2.1. Researching Opportunities and Threats

2.1.1. PEST Analysis

In business, knowing what is coming is the key.

Every morning when you're leaving the house, do you look out the window to check weather conditions? And if you're planning a big trip, do you check the weather forecast for the coming days?

On a macro level, a company would start with identifying a «Big Picture». Changes in your business environment can create great opportunities for your business – and cause significant threats.

For example, opportunities can come from new technologies that help you reach new customers, from changed government policies that open up new markets, or from social changes such as the increase of a retired population willing to relocate to your specific market. Threats can include deregulation that exposes you to intensified competition or a shrinking market due to political instability with certain countries.

PEST Analysis is a simple and widely used tool that helps you analyze the changes in your environment in the following categories:
- **Political**
- **Economic**
- **Sociocultural**
- **Technological**

This helps you understand the «Big Picture» forces of change that you're exposed to and, from this, take advantage of the opportunities that they present.

Figure 2-2:
PEST Analysis

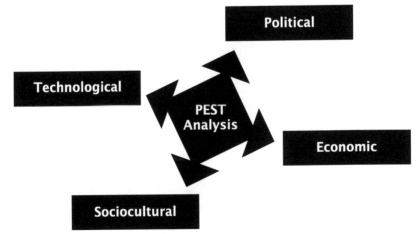

Start with PEST Analysis for the following reasons:

- It helps you to spot business or personal opportunities, and it gives you advanced warning of significant threats.
- It reveals the direction of change within your business environment. This helps you shape what you're doing so that you work with change, rather than against it.
- It helps you avoid starting projects that are likely to fail for reasons beyond your control.
- It can help you break free of subconscious assumptions when you enter a new country, region, or market, as it helps you develop an objective view of this new environment.

> *Do you see any trends in your market that you should be aware of as your threats or – more importantly – opportunities?*

In the table below, list at least two trends, changes, factors, or facts that may potentially affect your business environment.

Figure 2-3:
PEST Analysis of Your Market

PEST Environment	Research and List Trends, Changes, Factors, Facts
Political	
Economic	
Sociocultural	
Technological	

> *To be a well-informed professional agent, a Realtor should engage in essential Marketing Research based on the principle «from global to local».*

Start from the global overview of world events and trends, especially if your primary target market is an international community, and then shift to local content:

- Sign up for all key community media publications – local newspapers, blogs, social-media channels, and so on.
- Subscribe to blogs of the market's key players that you respect and value.
- Set up notifications for topics of your interest.

In Figure 2-4, make a list of the resources that you'll be tracking on regular basis.

Figure 2-4:
Global versus Local Informational Resources

Global Resources	Local Resources
Fill in Your Answer	
TV Channels	TV Channels
Publications	Publications
Blogs	Blogs
Online Specific Content	Online Specific Content

2.1.2. Applying PEST Results into SWOT Analysis

You've completed the first step of the business homework. The second logical step is to apply findings of the PEST Analysis into your SWOT Analysis Matrix.

In other words, trends, changes, factors, and facts discovered during PEST Analysis become your Opportunities and Threats of SWOT Analysis.

2.1.3. Taking Advantage of Opportunities through an Action Plan

By doing PEST Analysis you're now able to complete the other half of the SWOT Analysis by summarizing key business **Opportunities** and **Threats**. It's important to point out that both opportunities and threats are **external factors** of the business environment and pretty much not within your control. Therefore, it's imperative to identify these shifts and adapt to them.

Think of a relevant action that your business may take in order to take advantage of the opportunity, avoid risks, or minimize threat.

Ask yourself these questions:

- Which trends, changes, factors, and facts from Figure 2-1 should I take advantage of?
- What will it financially entail?
- Will I need to develop a specific website?
- Will I launch an advertising campaign?
- Will I approach specific key players who might introduce me or refer business to me?

Figure 2-5:
SWOT Analysis Part II—External Factors:
Opportunities and Threats

SWOT Factor	Your Business Opportunities	Your Action
Opportunities = Favorable conditions on the market	*Fill in Your Answer*	
What opportunities are available to you? **What trends can you take advantage of?** **How can you turn your strengths into an opportunity?**		Take advantage of opportunities

Threats		Fill in Your Answer
What is your competition doing? What can get in your way? What threats do your weaknesses expose you to?		Be aware of threats Anticipate the change

2.2. Spotting Your Target Market

Please note that for the purposes of this book **Target Audience, Target Market,** and **Target Niche** will be used interchangeably. However, in marketing theory, they have slight differences in definitions and application that are critical when developing communication strategy. Your target audience is the people who you want to know about you, such as

- **potential buyers and sellers** – the final service users;
- **referral partners** – other related industries who service the needs of the same type of client; and
- **influences and key players** for whom your reputation may be critical – other agents, managers, corporate partners, associations, and networking groups.

> *The real estate industry is unique in that it's a people business. The goal of Personal Branding is to market you as a Brand Personality.*

Don't limit your target audience only to the final users of your services, buyers and sellers. Think broader in terms of people who need to know about you as listed above. You need to market your personal brand to these people so that your brand has a direction.

Top producers specialize or target specific **Market Niches** that they are passionate about and will become the **Go-to Experts** in. Their specialized market focus is either a **Geographic** or **Demographic Niche**. They are perceived as dynamic, memorable resources in their market. This perception is the result of continual and consistent branded message and action.

By successfully applying branding principles and authentically aligning yourself with your selected client niche, you can build a successful brand.

Again, real estate is a people business. It takes real commitment of passion and effort.

Focusing on a market of people, places, or things that intrigue and excite you will change real estate from being a job to being an awesome, rewarding career. It's much more effective to work smarter than the traditional «work harder». In order to do so, it's essential to be passionate about what you do.

2.2.1. Crafting Your Ideal Clientele Profile

You need to define your potential customers using **characteristics** such as

* **lifestyle**
* **occupation**
* **geographic location**
* **income**
* **family life-cycle stage**

Figure 2-6:
Segmentation Dimensions

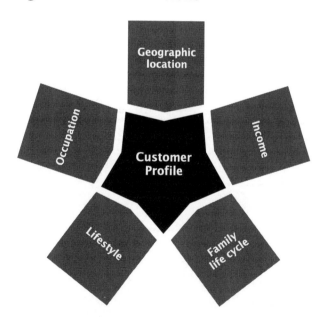

For example, you have selected to «farm» a gated community that offers an active lifestyle for a certain age group. You can become an expert by targeting buyers who are interested and excited about living in that community environment and sellers who are living in those communities.

«*First work on branding yourself and worry about prospecting and lead generation. Building relationships and being in the field makes a huge difference. Real estate is governed by the law of farm; you reap what you planted.*»

- Mark Hughes,
Branded Agent: The 7 Strategies of Top Personal Real Estate Brands

2.2.2. Being «First at the Table» When Targeting Future Customers

Real estate is not an instant-gratification type of business. There are certain business patterns and cycles; and this is not just a numbers game but a game which has several rules:

- **Passionate Attitude** – when you don't treat your business as a job
- **Patience** – going fishing daily doesn't always result in bringing in big fish with regular consistency, at least at the beginning
- **Presence** – you have to be accessible twenty-four seven in one form or another: yourself, through your assistant, with the help of electronic tools, and so forth.
- **Responsiveness** – answer your phone, come up with solutions, facilitate
- **Reliability** – deliver what you've promised
- **Responsibility** – value first, reward second

In addition to the above-stated rules, being the first one to try something new and different is challenging and risky like in any game; however, being a front-runner could be extremely rewarding.

For example, in my own real estate market, when Miami sales picked up and the interest from Brazilian buyers increased, one agent organized VIP parties where he presented several properties. He always sold at least one property during an event.

2.2.3. Researching Your Target Markets

What do you need to know about your target market? The answer is, you need to know everything. First of all, are you able to define your client profile? Try to complete the Client Profile Checklist in Figure 2-7 for all your target markets.

Figure 2-7:
Client Profile Checklist

Question	Profile
	Fill in Your Answer
Where do they currently live?	
What is their moving pattern?	
What is their family life cycle?	
What is their budget?	
What is most important to them?	
What lifestyle do they maintain?	
How do they socialize?	
What is their sphere of influence or behavioral group?	

2.3. Identify Your Fishing Spot

Your Fishing Spot, that is, Farm is a market niche that is uniquely yours.

Your Fishing Spot exists in the intersection of various pieces of your life:

• **Your «whys»:** your purpose or life mission

- **Your identity:** your skills, talents, and personality
- **Your target market:** the people you want to work with
- **Your offering:** the ideas you have to share

Finding your Fishing Spot allows you to stay true to yourself, and it gives you direction to form a strategy for developing your niche.

2.3.1. Knowing Everything about Your Niche

The most important marketing question is, how can your niche be reached? Building your target audience list is a research project on its own; therefore, get organized before completing this task.

Make a list, develop a database, set up files and folders, and make the best use of the information you have in the most suitable organizational system you're used to. Some people may treat this step as boring. I suggest you have the attitude of an explorer while in the investigation process. You're learning not only who your clients are but also – more importantly – how to reach them. Here are a few tips to help you organize this information:

- **Design compatible systems.** For example, set several Excel spreadsheets into a single file and devote each sheet to a specific type of potential client or classifying lead. You'll save so much time if you need to merge information (just be sure to be consistent with the table formatting).
- If you use any CRM (Customer Relationship Management) platforms in which you have to initially input data, always remember: «Junk in, junk out». **Be consistent with the minimum information required for input.**
- Your database is a potential goldmine. If it's initially done properly by setting up categories, campaigns, and schedules, then in the long run the time spent will pay off. Then **your task is to work the system and let the system do the bulk of the work for you.** A database is the foundation on which to build a solid brand because the brand has to be consistently communicated to the target audience to establish recognizable repetition.

2.3.2. Owning Your Niche

The ownership of your target niche will come to fruition only when you're able to create your desired reputation and following among your chosen target audience.

It's more efficient to commit to a few channels of your presence, interaction, and contribution than to try to be everywhere.

Owning your niche means you're creating a mini kingdom where you're a king or a queen of a particular target market. When people think of that niche, they think of you. The niche and your personal brand become synonymous and interchangeable.

You can create your own niche by picking a specific area that you want to be great at and claiming it. Ask yourself which problems you are especially good at solving, or who seems to be drawn to you. It may actually be an easy and obvious choice for you.

> *Don't be afraid to specialize on the niche! Let go of the idea of serving everyone.*

You can't be great in everything. And good is the enemy of great. Many agents are afraid to lose a lead so they take them all, and then they never find the time to focus on a specific type of client, area, or community. Because they're afraid of narrowing down their target audiences, they'll always be so broad that it'll be hard to define their expertise. Don't worry; once you master a niche through an established system, you always have the choice to grow and expand to new territories and client niches.

Avoid not being known for anything. Remember, system first, expansion next. Just imagine how much easier it is to duplicate success if you have already walked the walk and talked the talk. Then you'll be able to delegate and outsource some activities.

It doesn't mean that you turn down clients who are outside of your niche, but that you make it known to everyone that you especially love to work with a certain niche. Narrow your niche to one or two choices, and then start learning everything you can about your target audience. Investigate with the help of questions like those in Figure 2-8.

Figure 2-8:
Target Niche Questions

Question	Fill in Your Answer
What are sales trends in this neighborhood?	
What is the turnover rate?	

| What are the community newspapers, meetings, and events? | |
| What other related service providers work the same niche? | |

Establish yourself as an expert in that niche market. Become a subject-matter professional and the ultimate source for your niche, and enjoy serving it. The great news is that specializing makes it easier for you to function on a daily basis because you can predict behavioral pattern and react faster. Be the best «dancer» on that floor – blog, speak, socialize, and interact to be recognized in that niche.

2.4. Knowing Your Competition

One of the key steps, when working on your personal brand, is to understand who does the same type of work that you do, where you fit among them, and how you can better identify your uniqueness. In other words, know your direct and indirect competitors.

> *Your first task in observing your competition is to identify how your competition communicates its value to its target audience.*

With that information in hand, you can begin to identify what makes you different from your competition. Ignoring competition is a big mistake. Treat prominent competition as your free educational and training resource. In order to quickly learn from them, answer the following questions in Figure 2-9.

Figure 2-9:
Competitor Analysis

Criteria	Competitor A	Competitor B	YOU
		Fill in Your Answer	
Who do they serve?			
Strengths – What do they do well?			

Weaknesses – What do they do poorly?			
How do they market themselves? What do they do differently?			
What is their positioning and message?			
Which events do they attend? How do they network?			
Who is following them?			

After completing this table by including the information about your competitors, describe yourself against them. You may discover certain things that you thought were obvious, but they can really serve as grounds for building a competitive advantage. Once again, remember you're not an ordinary Realtor; you're an extraordinary brand.

Your goal is to learn from the best practices of your competitors. Become their follower. Use their resources. As they already spend money on those resources, take advantage of the available free information. Then look into opportunities that your competitors might have overlooked. It's an exercise of aligning the market segmentation with the existing competition and discovering gaps for new niches or understanding the potential for the large existing markets and why to focus on either one.

2.4.1. Researching Your Direct and Indirect Competitors

Think about your competitors, both actual and potential. What do they all have in common? You must have certain qualifications to perform in the real estate industry, and being similar to your competition is actually a good start. Therefore, set your mind to be a sponge for the first 90 to 180 days, either as a new agent or as you work to rebrand yourself. This is an expected time frame in which to actually be able to demonstrate your potential and gain as many technical skills as you possibly can. It's your probation period. But as you build on what you know, your similarities to your competitors become fewer and your differentiation becomes more apparent.

When you do the same things as your competitors, without differentiation, you become a commodity. Commodities are items based on price and not differentiation. Being a commodity doesn't give you any leverage. Your marketing objective is to distinguish yourself as a sought-after brand because when you're differentiated, people will pay a premium to work with you. Premium in this case isn't necessarily higher commission but higher valuation of your resources and time.

Your goal is to pick, define, highlight, package, and communicate your own unique promise of value. Your differences allow you to be heard. Think about whether or not your competitors' weaknesses will create an opportunity for you to shine. Think of the opportunities you'll have when people start talking about you, but don't interpret it as a bragging exercise. While making up this list, don't think of only tangible certificates or obvious skills but soft skills as well. For example, «I get things done in the most creative fashion.»

At the beginning you may not have many differences from your competition. Start thinking about how you can communicate your story in a different way. Something as simple as a sense of humor can be a differentiator.

You may pursue different directions, such as choosing to focus on a very defined and narrow niche, so that you practically don't have any rivals. Or you might cooperate and team up with another strong agent and cover a larger market by sharing resources. The questions below will help you review your competitors as well as analyze industry role models.

Figure 2-10:
Developing Tactics to Compete

Area	Your Tactic
	Fill in Your Answer
What are your competitors missing? **Is there a gap in the services that they provide that could be an opportunity for you?**	
If you're targeting the same area, what tactics do they use? **Which stactics are effective?**	

If you were their customer, what would the experience be like?	
How do they find their opportunities? What are the key learning points you can take away from their experiences?	
Are you trying to occupy the same space as someone else who has done it longer and better? If so, what new angle can you add to gain a competitive edge?	

For a real estate agent, competition means three business aspects:

- Which agents, if any, are **farming the same geographic area**?
- Which agents have clear **positioning** similar to yours and are appealing to the same market niche?
- What are the most probable **pipelines** your competitors have? What are their primary client sources?

The good news is that very few agents actually know the value of the above items – but now you do. Therefore, with this insight you are able to establish your target niche much faster and equally with other agents, who have been working that market for a longer time.

2.4.2. Tracking All Relevant Channels

Consider these other sources to learn more about your competitors:
- **Facebook business pages**
- **Industry websites, newsletters, newspapers, video channels, blogs**
- **LinkedIn groups and question panels**
- **Professional associations**
- **Industry leaders' Twitter accounts**

> *Study your competition in depth, and don't be afraid. If your market has a competitor, it means that you have identified a place that attracts others.*

Personal Branding helps you to define, package, position, and communicate the message of who you are in order to compete.

2.4.3. Overcoming Your Fears

Personal Branding involves taking your authentic self out into the world. You might face a fear of «What if no one wants my brand? What if I can't compete?» You might rarely hear this, but it's real in most people's minds. Self-esteem and personal confidence are the backup of your personal brand. The most important thing is to stay true and consistent with your brand through strategy:

- **Communicate better than anyone else**. Build your brand loyalty by being a great communicator.
- **Don't say yes just to agree.** Great brands stand for something, and when you're called to do so, stand up for what you believe in.
- **Have a great attitude.** Be known for your good nature and for being pleasant to work with on any level of relationship – with your colleagues, partners, managers, and clients.
- **Play fairly.** Focus on your reputation and long-term goals, not short-term gains. Don't be a deal chaser.
- **Overdeliver.** People like and trust reliable people, especially when they always receive value.
- **Become detail oriented and involved in the issues.**
- **Stay genuine and authentic.** You know who you are. Don't be afraid to be that.

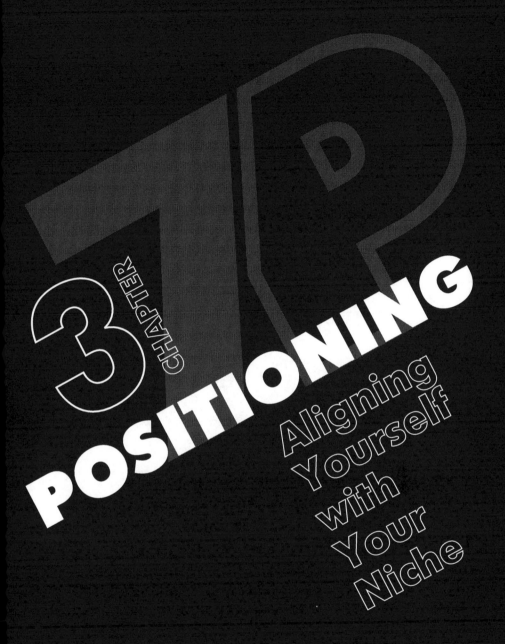

CHAPTER 3

POSITIONING

Aligning Yourself with Your Niche

3 POSITIONING
Aligning Yourself
with Your Niche

The third P of the Branding Model – **POSITIONING** – focuses on designing your message to establish your desired image among your potential clients.

Figure 3-1:
Chapter 3 Summary

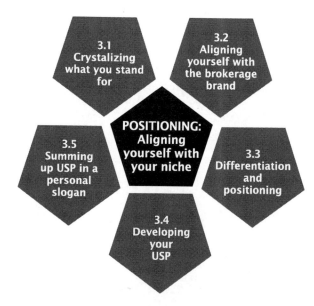

3.1. Crystalizing What You Stand for

3.1.1. Segmenting Your Market

After you define and research your target market, you want to make sure that your actions are in sync with your niche's needs and expectations. While researching and outlining characteristics of your target market, group all your findings into two broad categories:

- **Demographics** – statistical characteristics of a population such as gender, race, age, family life cycle, educational background, employment status, homeownership, and location.
- **Psychographics** – characteristics that describe consumer lifestyles, likes, dislikes, activities, interests, and opinions.

Market segmentation is a marketing process that involves dividing a broad target market into subsets of consumers, businesses, or countries who have, or are perceived to have, common needs, interests, and priorities, and then designing and implementing strategies to target them. Those subsets, also called **market segments** or **niches**, have to be heterogeneous enough to be separated.

The real estate purchase behavior largely depends on two primary consumer characteristics: the stage of the family life cycle and income. Other characteristics will further shape the Customer Profile.

> *The more detailed your Customer Profile is, the more targeted, focused, and cost efficient your marketing will be.*

For example, suppose you decide to target certain gated communities. Your Customer Profile description may look like: most of the residents are around forty-five to fifty years old, 70 percent are home-based entrepreneurs, and 75 percent of households are families with at least one child attending private school.

3.1.2. Appealing to Your Niche Both Rationally and Emotionally

Researching, knowing, and owning your niche is only half of the journey; you have to also lay a strong foundation for your target market to get attracted to you. Your target market will be attracted to you for different reasons. Rational attributes are solid qualities that people trust and depend on in you, whereas emotional attributes are often the reasons people want to be around you.

> *By using your attributes that are most valuable to the client, you'll be able to appeal to your target audience.*

The people who will be interested to work with you, hire you, or refer an important contact to you will first want to know if you have what it takes to do the job. In ordinary circumstances, in order to be hired, you must be able to demonstrate that you have the right education, experience, certifications, and skills to do what they need you to do. These are rational tangible qualities and skills for which you get paid.

Emotional attributes, on the other hand, such as sense of humor, empathy, and friendliness, are the qualities that appeal to your target audience, attract them, and make them want to do business with you. Having strong emotional attributes creates loyalty, and it serves you well when your target market has a choice to work with someone else. It's all about comments such as «He has such a great personality» or «She is always so classy.» Likability, personal charm, and charisma are the keys of a strong emotional bond between Realtor and client.

The uniqueness of the real estate industry is that anyone over eighteen years old, of any background and previous experience, can breakthrough into the business. There is no corporate ladder to climb, and there is no qualification designation based on your experience. It's all about who you're focusing on and how well you're positioning and presenting yourself to your target niche.

3.1.3. Highlighting Your Attributes to Your Target Market

Emphasizing your rational attributes is the starting point in positioning your value to your target market because you can back them up with tangible evidence of degrees, certificates, or work experience and track record. This is when you ask yourself the following questions:

* What special attributes/benefits do you offer to your clients?
* How will they benefit from it?

Put your clients' needs first. In other words, you define or invent your message based on why they should choose you instead of another agent. A great example of this is an agent's message stating, «You only list once with me». Always keep clients' needs at the forefront of your mind while you're defining your target audience and developing your message.

> «*Personal Branding isn't about being famous; it's about being selectively famous. It means knowing who needs to know you and being ever-visible to them. To this group you're a leader, an inspiration, a resource. To the rest of the world, you're completely unknown.*»
> -William Arruda

3.1.4. Creating an Emotional Bond: Investing in Relationships

Personal Branding is all about communicating your message to the right people. You're remembered by others through your actions, accomplishments, and the emotional connections you make. Personal Branding also requires consistency in behavior so that you're predictable, reliable, and therefore inspire trust.

Again what will people actually remember when they interact with an individual or service provider? The research study conducted in services marketing indicated that if you're asked to recall situations of interaction or service encounters with the service provider, you'll most likely recall only either extremely positive or extremely negatives ones. In other words:

Customers don't recall situations with adequate service in which their perceptions matched their expectations. They only recall circumstances in which their expectations and service promises have been exceeded or underdelivered.

The marketing concept of the Product Levels has already been brought to your attention in Chapter 2. A typical agent will produce a service on the Expected Level, which means the agent will only meet customer expectations. In order to impress, delight, and – as a result of these reactions – be remembered, you need to work beyond the Expected Level. The Augmented and Potential Product Levels are your room to come up with creative ideas and solutions to improve, grow, differentiate your brand, and, by exceeding customer expectations, create a long-term bond.

You can't build a solid brand without long-term relationships and customer loyalty, but building relationships doesn't come easily to everyone. In your personal life, how many good friends can you count? Try to stay away from the goal of becoming close friends with all your clients. Like in personal life, there are levels of relationships with people in the real estate industry. The most important is the system and action plan that will promote and maintain these relationships. Recommendations on how to take advantage of technology in order to assist you in the process of maintaining these relationships will be discussed in Chapter 6.

In Figure 3-2 try to list your action ideas for the respective relationships: from traditional updates and announcements to exclusive invitations and kids' events.

Figure 3-2:
Types of Relationships and Actions to Take

Relationship Type	Your Action
	Fill in Your Answer
Past Client	

Present Client	
Referral Agent	
Industry Partner	

3.2. Aligning Yourself with the Brokerage Brand

As a licensed professional, you have at least the following five possible alternatives when placing your license with brokerage:

- Be an agent within a well-recognized corporate brand.
- Be an agent within established local brand.
- Be an agent of niche boutique brand.
- Be an owner-broker brand.
- Be an agent of a large online brokerage brand.

Each framework has its advantages and disadvantages from a marketing point of view. The summary is presented in Figure 3-3:

Figure 3-3:
Comparison of Brokerage Scenarios

Brokerage Alternative	Advantages	Disadvantages
Well-recognized corporate brand	• High brand awareness • Branded materials at the cost of the brokerage • Corporate public relationship support • Training	• Smaller commission split • Explicit branding guidelines • Limited personal attention • Potential lack of teamwork
Established local brand	• Focused marketing approach to farm area, neighborhood, community • Larger commission split	• Fewer financial resources • Territorial limitations

Niche boutique	• Good for experienced agents	• Lack of branding support • Lack of training
Owner-broker	• Full control of financial resources	• Lack of corporate public relationship and marketing support
Online brokerage	• Minimum commission split	• Lack of personal support

Each agent when choosing brokerage type should take into consideration his or her own marketing skills as well as how much, if any, marketing and branding will be created for him or her.

3.3. Differentiation and Positioning

Differentiation is the result of the efforts taken to make a product or brand stand out as a provider of unique value to customers in comparison with its competitors.

Positioning is a marketing strategy that aims to make a brand occupy a distinct position, relative to competing brands, in the mind of the customer.

Creating your Personal Brand Profile is the process of combining what you know about yourself and what you know about your target market and competition.

Creating your Personal Brand Profile is like putting together a puzzle about yourself in order to see the real picture, the real you in the real environment. The outcome is clarity of your motivation and who you want to know about your brand and how others are already communicating to the same target audience. In doing so,

You bring to light your unique promise of value, which allows you to formulate a Personal Brand Statement/Positioning Statement, called a Unique Selling Proposition (USP), and develop a strategy to market your brand.

The USP is the factor or consideration presented by you as the reason why the service you deliver is different from and better than that of the competition.

Before you can begin to offer your service to anyone else, you have to sell yourself on it. This is especially important when your service is similar to those around you. Very few businesses are one of a kind. Just look around you: how many clothing retailers, hardware stores, air-conditioning installers, or electricians are truly unique?

> *Unless you can pinpoint what makes your business unique in a world of homogeneous competitors, you can't target your marketing efforts successfully.*

Your USP is extremely important to your branding success. Although it may be only a few words long, this statement expresses what you stand for, and it guides you in making decisions that are «on brand» for you so that you never veer off into activities that are «off brand». Your Personal Brand Statement keeps you energized and focused on meeting your goals.

> *Your USP is the heart and soul of who you are and what motivates you.*

Your USP is about relevant personal brand positioning and consistent exposure. It's about passionate execution of your service for the target market. Top production (Market Share) becomes very attainable if you're positioned to be the agent that your market thinks of first (Share of Mind) and chooses to work with (Share of Heart). Most clients (75 percent of the market) will use one agent that they decide to call first. So how do you become the agent who gets that first call? How do you become the agent who comes to mind first?

Buyers and sellers can easily research which agent has been in business the longest or who has the most designations and only work with him or her, but the reason most people call a particular agent is much less diligent. There is a huge communication gap at play that any agent can fill.

To be the agent who gets that first – and usually only – call, you position your personal brand to subtly engage and persuade sellers and buyers by appealing to their emotions.

To summarize the Positioning process:
- **Define your target niche.**
- **Design your unique promise of value** by answering the question, why should someone choose you rather than any other Realtor?
- **Name your direct competitors** and specify their online and offline presence and strengths (website, blog, events, etc.).
- **Develop your USP.**

3.3.1. Compiling Your Personal Brand Profile

You're the author of your own life, hopefully the one who will leave footprints and a legacy for those who follow you. Personal Branding gives you clarity to create your own story, live it, and then tell that story to the right audience. Stories are personal and emotionally connect with the audience, and nothing builds your brand better than a good story. With your story in hand, you can craft a winning biography and be prepared to offer an engaging response whenever someone says «Tell me about yourself».

Telling a story is a way to build trust, and every brand wants you to trust what it stands for. When you tell a story to your target audience, you're creating a bond with that person. A story lets your listeners decide for themselves whether they will trust you and the brand you're presenting. The objective of your story is to illustrate who you are; it should be an expression of your life.

3.3.2. Assembling All Personal Elements Together

Each of your characteristics is like a piece of a quilt. Each component is great; however, the whole beauty can be revealed only when all pieces are put together. Use Figure 3-4 to summarize all your personal characteristics – the building blocks of your brand.

Figure 3-4:
Personal Characteristics Summary

Category	Your Characteristics
	Fill in Your Answer
Needs	
Interests/Passions	
Values	
Education	

Work experience	
360 feedback	
Personality attributes	
Strengths	
Vision	
Mission	
Goals	
Target Niche	
Positioning	
USP	

Completing this table allows you to come up with a detailed description of the essence of your entire product/offering to prepare you for the next stages of the Branding Process: «Packaging» (Chapter 4) and «Promotion» (Chapter 5).

3.3.3. Putting Your Identity in Writing

When you're crafting a Personal Brand, consistency is your mantra. You want every marketing element to be recognized and associated with your style and to highlight your brand. This is a concern affecting your e-mail signature, outgoing voice mail, and every form of written communication.

Your marketing goal is to tell your brand's story with clarity so that you can engage your audience with your personality and your skills. In order to manage this aspect, follow these guidelines:

- Apply the principle of the **3 Cs** in all your communications: **communicate your message clearly, consistently, and constantly.**
- **Feature the same viewpoints, descriptors, taglines, and attributes** throughout all of your communication channels (oral, written, print, online, offline).
- Select **similar words** that show consistency in branding without being overly repetitive.
- Practice writing and talking about your brand attributes and strengths when talking about your work or discussing future plan. You must **have vision.**
- Foresee and try to understand potential problems and issues your target market faces or will face. **Offer solutions that highlight your brand.**
- Identify your target audience carefully and understand what compels them. Then reflect that information in your unique promise of value that speaks to your audience with relevance. Please note that **being relevant** is critical. For example, if you're emphasizing your service as being quick and that is not important for the client, then you're not providing any value to your client.

3.4. Developing Your Own Unique Selling Proposition (USP)

Now it's time to develop your own Unique Selling Proposition (USP), a promise statement that sets customer expectations. It sets the standards for your performance. It has to set you apart from the competition. You must be able to live up to your promise of value. Keep in mind that you're always better off underpromising and overdelivering to those you serve. Your brand promise is what you want to be known and remembered for.

Reread your Summary of the Personal Characteristics in Figure 3-4 and get a feel for your whole personality again; then develop your USP. It's your best-self version. Eventually it will emerge, but first you have to translate your thoughts into tangible promises:

- Select two to four words that quickly and clearly describe your **essential qualities.**
- Describe your **major strengths** that will be valued by your potential target niche.
- Define your **superstar factors**, which set you apart from your competition.

Keep in mind that your objective is to balance rational attributes with emotional ones. Therefore, select very descriptive adjectives and nouns for your statement. Remember, the USP isn't just for the external audience to build desired perception; it's first of all for *You* to help you stick to the brand you're creating and to deliver it in the best shape and form.

A **Personal Brand Statement/Positioning Statement/USP** is a promise of value that clearly differentiates you from competition. Positioning yourself keeps you in the minds of your target market and attracts the right people to seek out your expertise.

These are five steps to developing your own USP. Use Figure 3-5 to work through these steps.

Figure 3-5:
Developing Your Unique Selling Proposition (USP)

Stage	Fill in Your Answer
1. Define your target audience. (Who do you want to serve?)	
2. Figure out your frame of reference. (What is your point of view?)	
3. Identify points of difference. (How will you uniquely do this?)	
4. Offer support. (What makes you credible?)	
5. State your promise of core benefit. (Who? Where? Uniquely how? Why?)	

3.5.   Summing Up Your USP in a Tagline/Personal Slogan

A **tagline** or **slogan** is a phrase that follows your brand name and sums up your promise of value. It's short, precise, catchy, and memorable. It differentiates you in the minds of your target audience members, expresses your personality, and gives a sense of what you do. It's then used as an inseparable part of your logo on all your marketing materials, starting with your business card and e-mail signature and finishing up with video announcements. Marketing studies have indicated that use of eleven words or fewer is optimal to convey your message.

Some people use famous quotes as their taglines. Some people display a great sense of humor by using quotes or characters as their taglines; this certainly speaks of their personality. No matter what you've chosen, the most critical step is to align your unique promise of value with your personal brand and the needs of the target market, otherwise it will be confusing.

A well-done, strong slogan can be understood by anyone, even someone who doesn't know which industry you work in. Here are a few recommendations for slogan development:

- Google your phrase and see if anyone is already using it.
- If you intend to use your brand internationally, know how it will be translated into other priority languages.
- Keep it short in structure but broad in meaning.
- Make sure it's easy to pronounce.
- Try to use your unique characteristics to make it catchy.
- Write it in the present tense.

At this stage of the Personal Branding Process, you're ready to proceed to the Packaging and Brand Launch stages, where you will

- write your personal brand story – profile page, personal brief, elevator pitch;
- design an integrated communication plan;
- fashion up your brand;
- create your visual materials, packaging, and style – brand book; and
- determine your brand launch budget.

CHAPTER 4

7^P

PACKAGING

Designing Brand Identity

REALTOR BRANDING:
Marketing Yourself for **REAL ESTATE SUCCESS**

4P PACKAGING
Designing
Brand Identity

The fourth **P** of the Branding Model – **PACKAGING** – focuses on the **appearance** of your brand, the **physical evidence** of the brand, which creates the first impression. Unfortunately, you can't affect the customer using all six senses, but you can certainly influence his or her impression and decision-making process by the choice of the colors, fonts, and images you use to communicate with him or her.

By providing sophisticated input into this stage, you create a first impression and set the promise, which you then carry on and deliver upon in the personal interaction. Packaging is the service encounter in itself, and the client can interpret your brand as good or lousy based on your design – whether you're a professional or just a seasonal butterfly.

Figure 4-1:
Chapter 4 Summary

> *Your marketing objective is to develop a signature style, your special service pattern, that's uniquely mastered and offered by you.*

4.1. Designing Your Brand Name

It all starts with the name. When thinking of a brand name, a real estate agent has the choice of going by a

- **company brand name;**
- **personal brand name; or**
- **unique fictitious brand name.**

Each alternative has its advantages and disadvantages, which are addressed in Figure 4-2.

 Figure 4-2:
Considerations When Choosing Your Brand Name

Brand Name Alternative	Factors to Consider
Company brand name	• This option builds on the company's brand awareness, legacy, reputation, exposure, and corporate marketing efforts. • It lacks individuality.
Personal brand name	• It may be complicated for the name itself to become a sound brand. • It may be irrelevant to keep the name when the brand outgrows one individual.
Unique fictitious brand name	• A good name or domain name may help land a fortune.

Deciding on a great, memorable, and identifiable brand name can be a challenge for some individuals and a very natural process for others. Choosing a name for your business can be complicated because it's permanent – or at least should be. The brand name should capture the essence of your own company – you.

Below are six techniques to help you generate a memorable, meaningful, and unique brand name.

Figure 4-3:
Techniques to Generate Your Brand Name

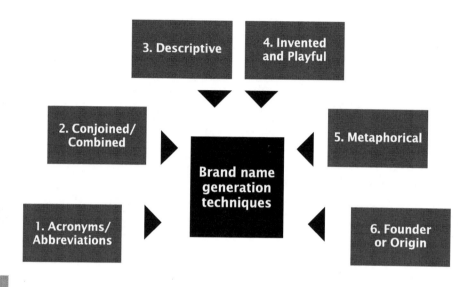

Figure 4-4:
Techniques to Generate Brand Name (Detailed)

Technique	Description
Acronyms/ Abbreviations	Some companies like to use long, descriptive names to identify who they are and what they do. Acronyms and abbreviations are often used to make longer names more friendly and easier to remember. In most cases, the customers are the ones who start using the acronyms for their own convenience.
	Example: RESF (Stands for Real Estate Sales Force)
	This method works particularly well if you have a long company name whose first letters of each word form a new, pronounceable word.

Conjoined/Combined	A conjoined brand name occurs when a brand name contains more than one word to form something new. Typically, the combined name gives two different meanings or understandings to the new word. It's a good alternative to an acronym, especially if you don't want to deliberately spell out what you do and still be clear and inventive. Example: EWM (stands for Esslinger-Wooten-Maxwell Realtors)
Descriptive	Descriptive brand names can effectively communicate what a brand does. On the downside, they are very hard, if not impossible, to get trademarked. The danger in choosing descriptive names is that the business sets itself up for confusion with competitors. Example: Miami Beach Team
Invented and Playful	Invented names can be quite fun and interesting to come up with. They can be playful, weird, or catchy – there are fewer boundaries and limitations. While descriptive brand names make it easy for potential customers to find your competitors, invented ones can make it difficult for them to find you. They demand much more marketing because they are harder to remember and less descriptive. Think about it – when Google first came about, I remember thinking to myself, «Hey, that is a pretty funny name, but what is it?» But a good marketing strategy (and loads of money) helped them emerge from under the woodwork. Example: The Twin Team
Metaphorical	The brand name could be based on the story of what the brand founders want their business to convey through its name. Typically, the stories are filled with emotional words or feelings relating to how they want their customers to feel or how they differentiate themselves from their competitors. Use names that embark feeling or emotion or have an underlying story or message. Example: Epic Realty

Founder or Origin	The majority of Realtors create their brands around their own names. While this method creates a name that is easily trademarked, it can create the same problem as invented names – we all can relate to the struggle of getting our names «out there».
	Example: Coldwell Banker (named after founders Colbert Coldwell and Benjamin Arthur Banker).

4.2. Directing Designer through Creative Brief

Now that you understand the importance of the **Brand Identity** stage, you should trust a professional designer to work on it. To ensure the best outcome from your relationship with a professional designer, you need to do your homework. Once you develop Brand Identity, it has to be carried through and adapted to all forms of communication. If you don't already have a designer, you can outsource freelancers from the following sites:

* www.elance.com
* www.logomojo.cm
* www.logodesignguru.com
* www.fiverr.com

A professional designer will start his or her work by asking you to complete a Creative Brief. A good **Creative Brief** usually covers the following items:

* **Brand and business:** A quick, two- to three-sentence summary is perfect.
* **Target audience:** The more detailed Customer Profile, the better.
* **Values to communicate through design:** What feelings and messages you want the visual design to communicate to your viewer.
* **Stylistic preferences:** Whether you want something artistic and bold or sophisticated and minimal, this is your chance to let the designers know.
* **Colors:** List your desired colors. Designers will give you visually appealing recommendations as well as take into consideration contrast and/or complementary color combinations.
* **Sample images:** One of the best ways to inform and inspire your designer is to provide images of other designs you like.
* **Additional comments:** Any special requests or comments.

Figure 4-5:
Sample Design/Creative Brief

Parameters	Fill in Your Answer
Company/brand summary	
Target audience	
Message, slogan, copy	
Mood, feelings, emotions	
Key images	Get sample images at www.shutterstock.com www.gettyimages.com
Stylistic preferences, fonts	
Colors	
Design style (samples, links)	
Additional comments	

Your output does depend on your input.

Garbage in, garbage out. Keep in mind that you're the Brand Visionary, and the designer's role is to execute and make tangible your vision. He or she isn't a freeform artist and must have a clear objective and description of your anticipated outcome.

4.3. Designing Your Logo

The objective of Branding is to make connections and engrave a stamp or leave a footprint in the audience's memory. The **Logo** is certainly a major element of any brand; it creates brand awareness. It can be a symbol, a text, a graphic, or a combination of these elements. Always keep in mind that people recognize, recall, and remember images more than text. First, the human brain recognizes and memorizes shape. Second, the brain interprets color. Finally, it interprets content and meaning of the words (Figure 4-6).

Figure 4-6:
Logo Perception

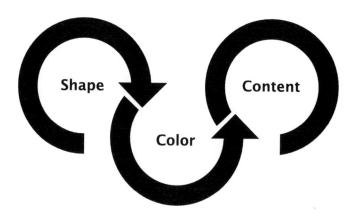

Your logo symbolizes your identity. In Personal Branding, it communicates your personality and emotional style. Your logo should be simple, clean, and unique. Figures 4-7 and 4-8 are your checklists for a well-done logo. Always remember that the ultimate test is if you like your logo, then you'll put it everywhere without hesitation.

Figure 4-7:
Logo Design Checklist

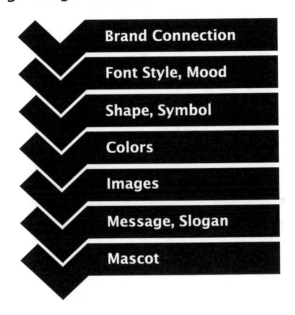

Brand Connection

Font Style, Mood

Shape, Symbol

Colors

Images

Message, Slogan

Mascot

Figure 4-8:
Logo Design Checklist (Detailed)

Parameters	Description
Brand connection	Think about how you would like everyone to emotionally connect with you. Find a **symbol** that will represent your personality and use it to connect with others.
Font style, mood	Your **logo font** is the analogy of your handwriting or personal signature. It's also the source of mood for the first impression. It can express professionalism, pricing level, a casual attitude, authority, creative flair, and so forth. Imagine you're trying to interpret a person's character through his or her handwriting – how do you wish your handwriting to communicate your qualities and characteristics? Small and precise? Structured and neat or illegible? Creative or formal? Impress – don't confuse – your audience by choosing appropriate fonts. It's an essential part of the logo

design process. Browse through www.myfonts.com to get sample fonts you feel may work for your brand. The first requirement when choosing a font is that it has to legible.

Fonts show mood and emotion, for example, a rounded font is more casual and relaxed than straight-line fonts, which communicate formality and trustworthiness. Heavy fonts show boldness, confidence, and strength while thinner fonts represent lightness and softness.

There are two font categories: Serif and Sans serif:

- **Serif fonts** have tops and tails at the ends of the letter strokes. These fonts are often used for print documents and are considered more classic-style fonts. Most books are printed in serif fonts because they lessen eye strain.

- **Sans-serif fonts** have a cleaner feel because they don't feature any extra marks at the ends of the letters. These fonts tend to have a more casual feel, and they have become the standard for online copy because they are easier to read on a screen.

Your choice of **brand fonts** will set your own distinctive signature style. Try to choose a maximum of three fonts and stick to them in all your communications: **Headline, Sub Headline, Body fonts.**

Shape, symbol	**The «Less is More» Rule** works in most branding-related artwork. As you've already learned in this chapter, the human brain recognizes and memorizes shape first. In order to identify a shape, a person doesn't necessarily have to be able to read, but in order to read, one has to be able to interpret shapes. Due to the fact that special and unique shapes are easier to remember, creation of such shapes is an essential part of the design process.
Colors	Color takes second place in the perception process, but it's still important because **color stimulates emotions.** Choose colors to not only communicate your brand but also to differentiate your brand from competitors. Color selection sends a powerful message and is key to representing your brand. Your brand color is a critical decision with regard to your visual Brand Identity. People do remember the color because they associate it with emotional content. Therefore, your color choice is critical in addressing

your personality.

The starting point when choosing the color for your personal brand is to understand which color(s) you're naturally drawn to, and then understand the meanings of different colors. A summary of color interpretation and meaning is presented in Figure 4-9.

Also review colors used by your competition. If everyone is using a teal color, it may not be the best differentiation strategy.

Apply your colors everywhere when appropriate: from your stationery to your car.

Images

Using your **Personal Image** in branding your marketing materials is a very traditional approach. There are several recommendations for you to follow:

- I would highly discourage you from using a personal photo on your business card because your chosen image may misrepresent you and set unrealistic expectations.
- It must be practically updated at least once a year.
- Don't waste space on your card; people won't remember you by your picture, but they will remember your personality through valuable conversation. (In some Asian cultures, the higher in the hierarchy that a person is, the less information he or she puts on his or her business card.)
- Make sure to choose an outfit to wear in your picture that communicates professionalism but is not too conservative. You're not working in the court; you're in the relationship business. On the other hand, sex appeal sells but not on real estate marketing materials.
- I would highly encourage the use of a variety of personal images on your personal website and social-media platforms, but be consistent with the main profile image(s) throughout all platforms and media to build Brand Recognition.
- You may also consider a set of images that will complement your style and communicate to the target audience. Always choose a dominant image around which other images will be consolidated. Emotional images may send very deep and comprehensive messages without having any physical wording.

- Also remember that images may add dynamics and perspective to the flat screen or cover page.
- The image has to tell a story.

Google yourself, and click on the Images tab. Have any of your images come up? Do you wonder how? The way it works is this: before posting your image from the computer to your website, blog, or social-media channel, name your image file using the key search words you would like the image to be associated with – your brand, personal name, and areas of your expertise.

Message, slogan	Your **slogan,** which you developed in chapter 3, is your **mantra** and therefore must be applied consistently throughout all communication channels and platforms along with your logo.
Mascot	Your logo can be complemented by a **mascot,** person, character, animal, item, or identity **graphic element**, which will be associated with your brand. In addition to your logo and slogan, you should add the power of a mascot character in creating your Brand Identity.

There are four simple tests you can use to evaluate your logo design before final approval:

- **Black-and-White Test** – Always design your logo graphics first in black and white for a simple reason: assuming that your logo is on a black-and-white photocopy, how will it look in its simplest execution?
- **Size Test** – Your logo has to look amazing, even tiny on a pen or huge on a billboard.
- **Color Test** – Try to play with contrasting colors and avoid any shading. Also, know exactly which colors you have selected as your brand Color Pantones in order to stay consistent with any application, print or electronic. The **Pantone Color Matching System** is largely a standardized color-reproduction system. By standardizing the colors, different manufacturers in different locations can refer to the Pantone system to make sure colors match without direct contact with one another. One such use is standardizing colors in the CMYK process. The CMYK process is a method of printing color by using four inks – cyan, magenta, yellow, and black.
- **Interpretation Test** – Run your logo by random individuals. Will they be able to interpret it the way you intended?

Figure 4-9:
Color Meaning and Interpretation

Color	Interpretation
Blue	Intelligence, wisdom, integrity, leadership, authority, truth, peace, loyalty, calming, communication, hope, imagination, reliability, confidence, clarity
Yellow	Sunshine, joy, independence, warning, vision, creativity, warmth, happiness, intellect, caution, light, self-motivation, independence
Green	Prosperity, rebirth, growth, nature, optimism, spring, change, fertility, relaxation, safety, luck, healing, environment, youth
Teal	Calming, confidence building, empathy, serenity, wisdom
Orange	Energy, optimism, competition, success, force, productivity, strengths, encouragement, humor, informality, vitality with endurance, determination, enthusiasm
Pink	Femininity, softness, love, warmth, friendship, children, affection
Peach	Stress relief, softness, gentleness
Red	Power, love, attention, activity, energy, desire, action, passion, determination, courage, vitality, enthusiasm, motivation, playfulness
Purple	Royalty, spirituality, inspiration, wealth, mystery, magic, dignity, luxury, ambition, personal power, intuition, self-worth, mental clarity
Brown	Solid, grounded, connected to nature, not luxurious, earthy
Black	Protective, strong, luxurious

Gold	Wealth, fame, decision-making clarity, sun, knowledge
Bronze	Wisdom, wealth, strength
Silver	Mystery, intuition, peace, moon
Gray	Elegant, classic, neutrality, well established
White	Purity, cleanliness, spirituality, openness, truth, refinement

4.4. Brand Book and Brand Identity System

Your marketing objective is to communicate your brand through all elements of physical packaging and evidence. In fact, applying your brand color consistently will ensure Brand Recognition. Real estate is a service industry, and to start creating a **Brand Identity System**, first, list all potential **Service Encounters** in your real estate practice.

A Service Encounter is any form of customer interaction with your brand, starting with your website and LinkedIn profile and finishing up with your car and office space. Each service encounter or **Service Touch** should reinforce the unique promise of value that your brand stands for. Technically you want to apply your own brand rules and principles from your **Brand Book** in everything you do and use them to create an integrated image through well-coordinated marketing materials. Your ultimate marketing goal is to differentiate yourself through all identity items, thus making your personal image recognizable.

In Figure 4-10 you'll find a summary of branding elements you would typically use throughout your real estate practice at different stages of the process, such as

- prospecting and customer relationship management;
- service delivery; and
- post-sale service.

Figure 4-10:
Brand Identity System Overview

PROSPECTING and CUSTOMER RELATIONSHIP MANAGEMENT
- Business cards
- Stationery
- Profile page, portfolio, brochure, presentation folder
- Postcards
- Creative Direct marketing
- Branded giveaways
- Website
- Blog
- Video
- Social Media channels
- Networking
- Conferences & events within the industry

SERVICE DELIVERY
- PowerPoint presentation
- SlideShare presentation
- Prezi presentation
- Sale signage, open house signage
- Open House day
- E-signature, auto responses
- Voicemail message
- Office interior design, your workspace
- Cutting-edge technology, cell-phone case

POST-SALE SERVICE
- Closing gift
- Relationship communications

Figure 4-11:
Detailed Brand Identity System

Branding Element	Marketing Tips
PROSPECTING and CUSTOMER RELATIONSHIP MANAGEMENT	
Business cards	Treat your business card as the quickest way to make an impression, not only visually but also through touch-and-feel impact. It can be a unique presentation of your personality and certainly you as a business. Below are few tips to consider: • In Figure 4-8 I have explained the reasons for avoiding the use of personal image on the business card. • I also don't recommend using unique size and shape formats. Initially, the unique size of the card may look like a creative idea; however, the chances of your card getting thrown away are greater than being kept simply because it doesn't fit into a traditional wallet or business cardholder.

- Keep your contact information clear. Don't put alternative phone numbers unless you're required by a broker to have an office phone. The reason is simple: anyone holding your card has to be able to quickly identify your number to call. The danger of having several phone numbers is this: imagine that a prospect calls the primary number, and you don't answer. Assume he or she dials the second number and is not able to reach you there, either. I guarantee the person will never call you again.
- Don't clutter your card with too much content and especially designations without any interpretation of what they stand for.
- The back of your card can be blank or used for your key Brand Image or explanation of your specialization and areas of expertise.
- While designing your business card layout and balance of its elements, keep in mind that the reader always focuses his or her attention on the largest object in any design. The larger the item, the more important the reader will perceive it to be.
- Lately, there is a trend of using a vertical layout design versus the traditional horizontal layout. Vertical layouts tend to be more distinctive.
- If you work with different language groups, I recommend producing alternative cards in different languages. Having one language on one side and another on the other side will be perceived as going cheap.

In addition to the business card design recommendations, I suggest reorienting your marketing tactics. Instead of having the goal of distributing your business cards, set a goal of collecting valuable cards and contacts. Then make the best use of proactive communication techniques and contact management databases.

Stationery

The primary business branding tools are as follows:
- letterhead
- envelope
- presentation folder
- address stamp
- mailing address stickers

All your tangible correspondence should incorporate brand colors, logo, and fonts.

It does make more sense to design all these elements as a package when outsourcing a designer. This package is called Brand Identity, Corporate Identity, Branding Package, or Brand Book.

Profile page, portfolio, brochure, presentation folder

Most real estate marketing tools have shifted online or transformed into some form of electronic media or application. However, profile pages, sales portfolios/ track records, personal brochures, and presentation folders are still very powerful traditional marketing tools. For a real estate agent, they aren't as much sales tools as they are image-building tools. It's still a very effective way to connect with your target audience.

Some brokerages might provide branded corporate marketing materials. However, if this isn't your situation, below are a few design recommendations:

- High-end clients appreciate high-quality design and print. The rule is, don't do your brochure in an economic fashion; high-quality design and printing are a must.

- Inspiring trust and building a respected reputation is the purpose of the brochure.

- Make the best use of superior design elements and images. Your cover must be eye-catching so that the reader wants to open it and discover more.

- When spending money on print, invest in quality paper. Keep in mind the touch-and-feel impact. The trend is to use matte, semigloss paper versus glossy paper, as well as thicker stock, which feels more expensive.

- Experiment with unique sizes and dimensions. Square brochures are perceived like invitations and are opened more often than rectangular ones.

- Highlight your unique promise of value in your brochure. Make sure that you convey your Personal Branding in such a way that it shares your emotional attributes. Use your biography to help the reader feel like he or she already knows you.

- Tell your story. Think about what makes you interesting. Tell it in third person, so that it doesn't make an impression of bragging.

Postcards	Thank-you cards, holiday cards, and invitations are another personal form of communication. We underestimate the meaning and impact of hand-written postcards nowadays. People do appreciate the time that you spend to sign the card and not just reply with a text message or e-mail.
	As with your brochure, use high-quality, heavy-stock paper. You can produce customized postcards at www.tinyprints.com, www.shutterfly.com, and www.picaboo.com, or purchase ready designs at: www.houseofmagnets.com/notecardcafe.
Creative Direct Mail	Traditional Just Sold/Just Listed cards aren't only direct trash items because of their message but also due to their form of communication and lack of consistency. Unless you're farming an area and are able to demonstrate a repetitive sales track record, using this type of direct marketing is a waste.
	Instead, if you're just starting, consider other creative forms of direct mail. For example:
	• At www.sendsations.com you're able to select a set of twelve cards that can be branded with your personal image, logo, and contact information and mailed once a month. The beauty of this direct-marketing tactic is the automation of your marketing campaign and engagement of the prospect into a series of collectable cards.
	• Another creative idea is to mail a gifted magazine subscription with your branded sticker. Once a month, your prospect will receive a top glossy magazine as a gift from you. https://cbrre-fl.magazineclosinggift.com/default.aspx
	In any direct marketing, always include your personal mailing address in the mailing list. This way, you'll be able to track and control the execution of your marketing campaign.
Branded giveaways	If you're practicing event sponsorships or have occasions when you distribute promo items, you can find thousands of branded opportunities at www.discountmugs.com.
	There are many more creative items that prospects or clients will find unique and useful beyond the traditional pen. The main criteria when choosing branded giveaways is what will make the clients keep them.

Website

Your online appearance is now even more critical than your hard-copy version. All your potential clients will first Google your name. Try to do a quick Google search test and see what comes up under your name.

- In order to corner a market niche, make sure to secure proper domain names. A good domain name, being a relatively small, immediate investment, may create a fortune. It's better to acquire all possible word combinations and even misspelled versions. The domains are inexpensive and can be purchased at:www.arbordomans.com, www.godaddy.com, or www.hostgator.com.

- Don't worry if you decide that a certain domain name is no longer of your interest and doesn't serve the purpose. Let it just simply expire, resell it, or even lease it.

- If still available, buy your personal domain name combination as soon as possible at www.yourname.com. If not available, play with a unique version of your name that later could be used as your professional nickname. If your name can be easily misspelled, always buy a potential misspelled version.

- If you're going after international markets, buy country-specific domains with common local extensions, such as .ru for Russia and .ca for Canada at www.101domain.com.

- As for the unique brand name, my recommendation is always buy all versions of it, for example, singular and plural. Or if by changing the order of the words in the name combination it still makes sense, buy a different order as well. www.godaddy.com has a convenient, built-in feature of generating related name alternatives if the name you were trying to get is no longer available.

- One place to find out who else is using your name is at www.knowem.com. This site looks to see who uses your name across various social-media sites. You can also visit www.howmanyofme.com to find out how many people online have your same name. The tool at www.vizibility.com creates a scannable code that allows you to point people to your sites even if you're not using your name. If you're still having difficulty with finding a strong domain name, make yourself visible by using professional credentials or your company name in your domain name.

- Make sure to carry consistent style and theme throughout your offline and online presence. Create a system that disciplines you in updating all your channels consistently. You most likely will have different communication channel preferences depending on different target audiences.

In online channels you might face a challenge of changing the fonts and color because different media have different technical requirements. For example, you might need to change the fonts for the website for better readability.

Blog

Blogging is one of the fast-track tools to rank your name higher in a relatively short time. Because www.blogspot.com and www.blogger.com are Google applications, your success with blogging will positively affect your Google ranking. Even if you don't have your website yet, always start at least by creating a blog in which your personal name, your domain name, and your brand name will be consistently used.

Video

YouTube is the number-two search engine following Google. Branding your videos through the consistent use of screenshots and even music intros is obvious but often omitted. Just think of your favorite TV show; isn't it the best example of consistency and Brand Recognition?

It's critical to take advantage of the video option, especially now when any individual may create and lead his or her own free broadcasting.

Planning a series of videos to engage your target audience into a series of relevant topics will encourage clients to subscribe to your channel. If you're outsourcing a professional video team, planning a series is great from a marketing point of view and a budget justification. You can definitely get a better rate per video and at the same time have a logically integrated marketing campaign. Think of committing to producing regular video blogs (vlogs).

When shooting the video, consider a branded back-drop as your video background. If you're shooting video in open houses, you certainly shouldn't mix million-dollar properties with the less pricy homes on the same website.

The YouTube Capture application allows you to produce videos on the go.

When your videos are complete, put them permanently on your website and your YouTube channel and spread the link through social-media platforms.

People like the human side of the brand and trust it more. Video puts your humanity on display.

Social-media channels	LinkedIn, Facebook personal and business pages, Twitter, Instagram, and Pinterest use your name as well to build your brand. These channels are driving forces. You make a first impression online as much as you do in person; therefore, personalize and brand your social-media platforms.

Personalization of social-media sites can be done by simply

- customizing the background page;
- using brand colors; and
- having a familiar name/title for the page, logo, slogan, and certainly master personal image.

Whenever possible, try to mention your website by providing a link to relevant content when you're posting your own content or commenting on others'. Be selective with any visual content that will be associated with your name, such as images and videos you post.

You'll be surprised how small the world is, and you'll soon get to meet people in person who already know you from your marketing channels. This happens to me at conferences, the local gym, and at the grocery store.

Networking	Your Brand Identity is being created by you on a daily basis. Obviously you're consistently building Brand Image and reputation not only through your packaging but also through activities you engage in. Networking should be ranked the number-one branding activity for a real estate professional.

Being selective about groups and events you attend and how well you prepare for the «hunt» is very critical in the people business. In chapter 5 you'll get more tips on how not to work but to network.

Industry conferences and events	Establishing a clear reputation among colleagues and industry leaders is another building block for your brand positioning. Do your colleagues and partners even know what you specialize in? Will your name ever come up if need arises? A clear, consistent image among other Realtors can become a strong referral source.

SERVICE DELIVERY

PowerPoint presentation	If you're still a comfortable user of the PowerPoint presentation, brand your template. You'll look professional and well coordinated.
SlideShare presentation	SlideShare, www.slideshare.net, is an online platform in which you can share your PowerPoint presentations. It's also a highly searchable platform. It's not likely that anyone will buy through it; however, it's very likely that it will assist in ranking your name in Google as well as in positioning you as a go-to person in the subject matter.
Prezi presentation	If you want to make a more sophisticated impression with your presentations, a great alternative to PowerPoint is Prezi at www.prezi.com. Prezi presentations allow you to design more dynamic and interactive presentations in a very simple fashion, which can be shared as links, downloaded, and presented online as well as offline. You'll be able to integrate videos, images, and music on a beautiful presentation canvas.
Sale signage, open house signage	Real estate signs such as «For Sale» and «Open House» are tough places to brand yourself. Even though «For Sale» sign designs must meet industry, corporate, or city requirements, «Open House» signs may be more creative. How about promotion flags? They should get much more attention.
Open House day	All stationery items used on Open House days must be branded: property flier, brochure, pens, pencils, business cards, sign, signup sheet, water, candy, presentation DVD, neighbor invitations, broker invitations, giveaways, food service plates and utensils – creativity is endless. Think creatively about your own signature style to host Open House days, whether based on creative elements or grand approach. Pretend that it's your star hour, where you're the main performer on stage, and you're the film director and script writer. You might think of a unique theme and name for your event. Example 1: The Only Haunted Open House Example 2: Santa's Retreat

E-signature, auto responses	Your e-mail signature can reinforce your brand every time a person communicates with you. Observe others' e-mail signatures for the amount of content, fonts, and logo usage, and see what feels right. Please keep in mind that total absence of the e-mail signature is a complete branding failure on your part if you want to position yourself as a professional industry player.
Voice-mail message	Ideally each call should be answered within the third ring. However, that it not always possible, and in those cases, your voice-mail message is the first service encounter that you deliver. Remember you're a productive business person, and you're not too busy to be productive.
	A professional message can either attract and build immediate trust or scare customers.
	Avoid situations where your voice-mail box is full. You will lose any opportunity to interact with the client. Always think that each call is your next million-dollar call.
Office interior design, your workspace	Your brand extends into your physical office workspace as well as your portable workspace (your laptop, iPad cover, phone case, car).
	Everything that someone sees around you is part of your brand environment.
	The color of your stationery and office accessories are the easiest way to communicate your Brand Identity.
	Think about what makes your target audience comfortable and interested. For example, if you position yourself as a penthouse expert, books about contemporary architecture or rooftop gardens are relevant.
	Think of a unique item that reflects your personality, for example, a cup full of colored pencils.
	If one of the communication channels for your clients is Skype, make sure you have a nice, professional office background when you host Skype meetings, simply because details matter.
	A cluttered, messy office sends a signal about your organizational skills. «You never get a second chance to make a good first impression» applies to the work environment as well. Don't take anything to your workplace that compromises your credibility,

	including offensive or sensitive-content cartoons, religious content, very personal pictures, sexual humor, stuffed animals, or artificial flowers.
Cutting-edge technology, cell-phone case	If you're positioning yourself as a cutting-edge tech expert, make sure to have current equipment. Brand all your equipment and tools. Doing so shows attention to details and helps you appear up-to-date.
	If an agent worries about his or her physical age, there is no better way to appear up-to-date than by using the latest technology. It will actually be very noticeable and appreciated.

POST-SALE SERVICE

Closing gift	Think of the closing gifts as a cherry on top of the ice cream as well as value-added service to cement relationships. It's typically not expected; therefore, you have room to exceed customer expectations. The choice primarily depends on the target receiver. Make sure to take into account cultural differences in gift giving, especially interpretation of colors, values, and amount of items. Some customized gift ideas can be found at www.personalizationmall.com.

As you're moving forward with every single element of your Brand Identity, you'll be able to crystalize your image to yourself first. This in turn will allow you to confidently and genuinely present yourself in all your business endeavors.

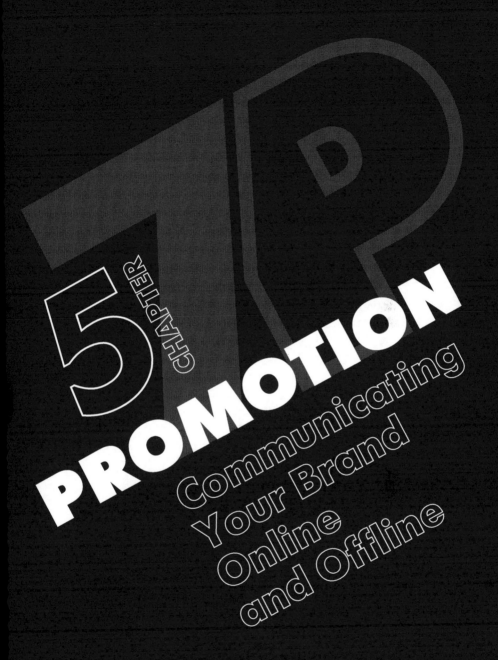

CHAPTER 5

PROMOTION

Communicating Your Brand Online and Offline

5 PROMOTION
Communicating
Your Brand
Online and Offline

The fifth P of the Branding Model – **PROMOTION** – focuses on communicating your brand.

 Figure 5-1:
Chapter 5 Summary

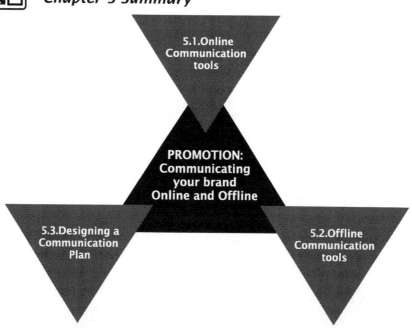

When you're clear about your personal brand, you want to communicate it in everything you do. In politics and show business, it's called **Image Making**. For you it means not only making sure that your online and offline communications reflect your brand but also paying attention to your actions, your dress style, your body language – in other words, every aspect of your communication. The bottom line is that only through relevant differentiated appeal and consistent message does a brand come to life.

For all online communications, it's critical to mention the importance of being very careful with overpromising through your online presence. Some agents develop fabulous websites, online presence, and communications. However, when you meet them in person, you get quite disappointed because of the contrast between the image portrayed and reality. Only genuine representation of yourself through all forms of communications – online, offline, in person – can create a strong personal brand.

Chapter 5 will systematize available marketing tools into your Integrated Marketing Communication System.

Figure 5-2:
Integrated Marketing Communication System

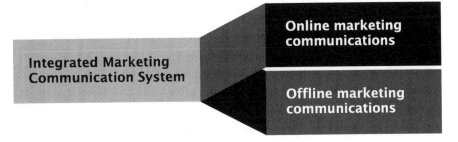

5.1. Online Communication Tools

First, let's start with online communication channels for your business. Depending on your own skills, decide which of the channels you're able to build and manage on your own and which ones you'll outsource. (See Figure 5-4.)

Figure 5-3:
Online Marketing Communication Tools

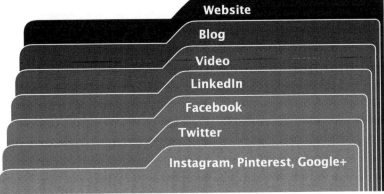

Figure 5-4:
Online Marketing Communication Tools (Detailed)

Channel	Marketing Application	Do It Yourself / Outsource
Website	• Online storefront (entrance) • Professional reputation	Outsource
Blog	• Announcer • News anchor	Yourself
Video	• Entertaining, educational, emotional, personal broadcasting	Yourself/Outsource
LinkedIn	• Professional resume/business profile • References • Referral source	Yourself
Facebook	• Personal and business media	Yourself
Twitter	• Just-in-time media	Yourself
Instagram	• Just-in-time media	Yourself
Pinterest	• Idea board • Vision board • Interest-sharing platform	Yourself
Google+	• Google improved local search visibility	Yourself

5.1.1. Website

Assuming that, after reading chapter 2, you were able to identify your target audience, you might consider several distinctive market niches that you feel like going after. In this case, your objective should be creating a **Master IDX Website,** which is your **online department store**, and designing several highly specialized **landing pages**, which will address the needs of your very narrowly defined customer niches.

Keep in mind that whether it's a full-scope real estate website with all kinds of different tools or a landing page, they both have to be promoted with proper

Search Engine Optimization (SEO). As an alternative to a landing page, which is a limited version of the website, you can consider building a specialized **blog** and link it to your website. A landing page and a blog serve as multiple doors to access your website. They are your shopping windows with their unique appeal.

Below is the summary of the minimum requirements needed to make your website a major business generator:

- Don't try to save on a good **logo** design. It's the first signal of your professionalism.
- Readability and user-friendly **interface**, **structure**, and **navigation** are essential for a strong real estate website.
- Make sure to have a **lead-capture** system built in.
- The website is a perfect medium to feature your **personal image**. In fact it could not be more appropriate; it does inspire trust when people know who they're dealing with.
- Enhance your website with a **personal profile video** in the form of a unique introduction. It will create an even more powerful presence.
- Position yourself as an expert by providing **resources that are of interest to your target audience.** Make sure that all hyperlinks work and that the clients are able to come back to your site and not be carried away. One way to do this is to open new content in a separate window.
- Integrate **social-media links** for all types of information that might be potentially shared.
- **Schedule to update your website on a regular basis.** Depending on the nature of your interaction with your target audience, it's recommended to review your website once a quarter. Your website is your reputation. How current it is shows your involvement.

Once you have launched your website, the main marketing objective is to promote it. You can certainly pay someone to do it for you. However, there are three tips that I have personally tested and recommend to start with them on your own:

- **Blogging** helps to promote the name of your website in Google search, assuming that your blog and your website have the same word combination.
- Make sure to request an access to the backstage of your website from your website developer. You'll be able to experiment on your own with your SEO by «playing» with key search words in the title, description, and metatags of your individual website pages. This is especially relevant if you have a specific language version when you're serving international clientele and you're the one who speaks that language.
- Get familiar with the **Google Remarketing Tool**. How does remarketing work? Have you noticed that after visiting certain websites, no matter where you go after that, the banner of that brand starts following you?

Remarketing as a paid form of advertising can help you reach people who have previously visited your website. You can even show these previous visitors ads that are tailored to them based on which sections of your site they visited. Your ads could appear to them as they browse other sites that are part of the Google Display Network or as they search for terms related to your services on Google.

5.1.2. Blogging

A blog is a primary conversational marketing tool for sharing updates and industry-related content, such as news, tips, and checklists. Audiences favor lifestyle-related content as well. Both industry and lifestyle content can project your image as an expert in a certain geographic area or type of properties.

The good news is that you don't have to be a professional writer or have web-designing skills to maintain your own blog. All you need is the initial setup of the design template to brand your page and the ability to write in a conversational tone. In fact, conversational tone is the major blog characteristic that differentiates it from professional news articles created by journalists.

Average consumers like to read blogs because of the simple language as well as the ability to comment on the content. Feedback and customer engagement is the key to keeping your potential clients interested in your blog.

From the SEO standpoint, quality blogging aids branding in these ways:

- **Building reputation through expertise.** Sharing information on regular basis is a foundation to being perceived as knowledgeable in the field. As a result of it, you might become the go-to person for the subject matter. You might be approached by journalists, other bloggers, authors, or conference organizers for an interview, presentation, or other forms of engagement.
- **Attracting other professionals** who value content in order to set up quality networking platforms.
- **Getting picked up by search engines.** The goal of any marketer is to make your profile come up in the top ten Google search results. Blogging is the tool that will come up in search results faster than any personal website, especially if the name of the blog contains the key search words connected to your targeted market. Regular posts, the right headlines, proper use of search key words (the words your potential audience is most likely to use), images, and good-quality, consistent content will help web crawlers pick you up and land you in the top search results.
- **Expressing your personality** by balancing business content with your own style. A blog is relatively easy to set up, customize, and manage. Be creative with content and its format by using visuals such as images and videos. Treat it as a long-term commitment; a blog has a slow but steady growth rate.

- **Creating discussible content.** Blogging fosters comments and shares. If the readership finds it hard to share, you'll lose the marketing angle. You must make sure you have built-in options to share the content via e-mail or through social media. By nature, people like to comment; it allows them to express their thoughts, opinions, and experiences.
- **Managing reputation.** Blogging is one of the public relations marketing tools used to manage reputation. The key is to try to be first with your interpretation of the story.
- **Establishing and growing your community** is one of your blogging objectives, and the best news about it is that it's free. Your regular readers/ subscribers become your **online community**, which supports you, advocates for you, and refers you. For you it's a tool to update the entire community with one click of a button – for free.

Stay away from the sales pitch. Go beyond the obvious, and people will likely read it.

5.1.3. Video

The use of video becomes more popular in the industry as technology becomes more sophisticated. To an average user, a good video is no longer a professionally done, expensive production.

The main reasons for committing to videos:
- YouTube is the second largest search engine after Google.
- Video gives the viewer a life perception of content without them having to read. Especially, in your international marketing efforts, video creates advantage over text content for various language groups.
- At this juncture, new technology videos taken by drones (Unmanned Aircraft Systems [UAS]) is definitely an advantage for promoting your business; however, federal and state regulations may prohibit or limit the use of such technology.
- Video can be used as an alternative to blogging (called Vlogging). If you're confident in front of the camera, you might consider Vlogging instead of blogging. For example, instead of e-blasting an electronic flier, consider using video Open House commentary. Keep in mind that there is some form of editing involved.
- Video builds brand awareness. Invest in high-quality personal videos. Your profile video can be added to your website and all other social-media channels. Your potential clients would like to «meet» their Realtor online first.

Unfortunately, videos about properties have very little chance of going viral. However, there are examples of great videos that generate a lot of attention and have great shareability. All those videos have one thing in common: they are entertaining. Therefore, in order to come up with attention-catching videos, try two different roles: marketer and journalist. And take the best of both professions:

- Be a marketer of the property.
- Be a marketer of lifestyle.
- Be a self-marketer (Profile Video).
- Be a news anchor for your target audience.
- Be an expert source of information.
- Be an announcer of new projects and events.

In all your videos, try to create value for your audience through

- inspiration
- entertainment
- education

Follow these minimum guidelines when creating the video:

- Determine if humor is appropriate.
- Keep it short (between thirty seconds and two minutes).
- Keep it engaging.
- Don't lecture; motivate.
- Deliver your messages early.
- Plan a video series.
- Include a call for action.
- Finalize your video post strongly with proper SEO: keywords, title, description, and tags.

If you don't feel comfortable taking a leadership role in the video, you could overcome that obstacle by becoming an interviewer. Here are some tips for interviewing on camera:

- **Do your homework well.** Know the subject of the interview. Create your interview questions or statements ahead of time and share them with the interviewee. Avoid closed-ended, yes/no questions. The viewers will get bored and switch to other videos.
- **Avoid any reading.** Your video presentation has to be as natural as possible. Practice talking to yourself in front of the mirror. Practice your speech by imagining that you're sharing exciting news with friends. It will be genuine, natural, and passionate if you're interested in your subject.
- **Pay attention to your body language and bad personal habits.** «Ums», coughing, and so forth are very noticeable on camera. Don't hold anything in your hands because it will make you more nervous.
- **Maintain eye contact.** Look either at the camera or the interviewee.

- **Or become an «invisible» news anchor** by reading the text on the video background.

5.1.4. LinkedIn

Why should you care about a strong professional profile on LinkedIn? At first you might think that the chances of getting a buyer or seller in the LinkedIn platform are low. And you're absolutely right! However, here are key reasons why it's extremely important:

- If LinkedIn is a professional «billboard», you better be there because you're in a professional business.
- LinkedIn has gained a reputation of being a multiservice professional business platform. For real estate professionals, this allows you to reach out to other professionals who serve the same target market as you, such as insurance agents, divorce and immigration attorneys, financial advisers and CPAs, jewelry dealers, art dealers, designers, and landscapers. Not only can you establish your virtual real estate team to serve all your client needs but you can also develop strong relationships for mutual referrals.
- Google ranks high a complete profile; therefore, when clients are googling you, they'll not land just on your casual media platform such as Facebook but also on the formal professional vehicle.

Try to avoid the following **common LinkedIn mistakes**:

- incomplete profile
- unprofessional, distracting profile photo, no photo, or no background image
- ineffective use of keywords and a boring, uninformative headline
- blank and ineffective summary section
- lack of descriptions and/or weak descriptions of job duties and accomplishments
- blank specialties and/or skills and endorsements sections
- lack of completed special sections
- lack of portfolio items in your summary and experience sections
- unutilized LinkedIn jobs functions
- insufficient or ineffective group membership
- lack of recommendations, very few recommendations, and/or boring or error-filled recommendations
- lack of consistency; discrepancies; no style in format and structure; and spelling, grammar, and punctuation errors
- unattractive formatting
- websites labeled generally – e.g., «Company Website» or «Personal Website»
- public profile URL (link) with lots of numbers, letters, and slashes at the end

- fewer than five hundred connections
- a static, unchanging, and outdated profile
- lack of alternative language profile

5.1.5. Facebook, Twitter, Instagram, Pinterest, and Google +

It is recommended to have presence by having active accounts on all social-media platforms. However, you should choose to focus on the ones which effectively reach your target market.

When deciding on the choice of specific social-media platforms, answer the questions provided in Figure 5-5.

Figure 5-5:
Choosing Social-Media Platforms

Question	Fill in Your Answer
Which platforms are used by the majority of your potential clients?	
Which platforms are being underestimated or underused?	
Which of the platforms listed in your answers above do you feel most comfortable using?	
What kind of content are you likely to share to build followship among your target market? (Specific social-media platforms are more appropriate than others.)	
Which platforms will result in greater customer engagement? (In the social-media terminology «engagement» stands for length of time and quality of interaction between a brand and its followers.)	

Figure 5-6:
Summary of Social-Media Platform Applications

Social-Media Platform	Application
Twitter	Tell 140-character stories, statements
Instagram	Share images and tips
Pinterest	Share tips and how-tos
Facebook	Share videos, links
Google +	Share video demonstrations, local content
LinkedIn	Use as blogging platform for professionals

All these platforms allow you to not only create content but – more importantly – share it, let your online community comment on it and spread it with just a click of a button.

It's important to distinguish the difference between customers and an online community. While customers are the people who use your services/products, community members are rallying around your brand for one reason or another. Your online community consists of the relationship circles shown in Figure 5-7.

Figure 5-7:
Relationship Circles

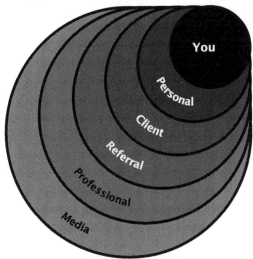

Figure 5-8:
Relationship Circles (Detailed)

Group	Representatives
Personal Circle	Family, friends
Client Circle	Present clients, past clients
Referral Circle	Industry colleagues, competitors, strategic business partners
Professional Circle	Professional associations
Media Circle	Media

Managing relationships with each of those groups must be done through relevant content that appeals to the interests of those groups. If ten years ago professional marketing efforts were managed by public relations manager through letters, newspapers and magazine articles, Event Marketing activities, and radio interviews, all these activities have now shifted online and spread with the speed of lightning.

Though community members may have different reasons to follow you (including your competitors tracking you for marketing research), overall most of them feel good about your brand and may collectively become a huge brand advocacy force and free word-of-mouth advertising.

Another great aspect of focusing to build a strong online community is that community means trust. The reason for inspiring trust is regular interaction of the brand with people. Also, a conversational mode of interaction doesn't feel like selling at all. Your community feels good about interacting with you, and therefore is more likely to «buy» from you or refer your services.

Last but not least, online community doesn't have set borders or time zones, and becoming truly international or global is just a matter of proper content. It makes it possible to develop great resources, partnerships, and collaborative synergies through global reputation.

For all online tools, follow these four rules:
- Establish your expertise by focusing on your unique set of skills and knowledge.
- Participate religiously but selectively in a conversational mode.
- Stay away from self-promotion and obvious selling techniques.

- Build your go-to-person reputation by providing valuable content and resources to your online community.

The power of social media is that long-term commitment will allow you to reap the fruits of your labor, and just one smart move can go viral like you never anticipated. Would you agree that strategically appealing to your relationship circles is extremely exciting and promising?

If you're just starting your real estate career, free social-media platforms are the only affordable advertising. Why not take advantage of them? Don't take them for granted and don't treat them as obvious. Very few professionals actually maintain these platforms consistently and with purpose. Therefore, design your own **Free Brand Launch Campaign** as detailed as you would a paid campaign.

Treat social media as part of your marketing job and don't fall into the addictive mode of using it just for the sake of socializing. It's all about **Return on Investment (ROI)**, where your biggest investment is time.

5.2. Offline Communication Tools

All offline tools are summarized in Figure 5-9 below.

Figure 5-9:
Offline Marketing Communication Tools

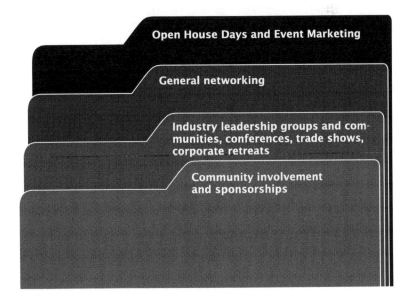

Open House Days and Event Marketing

General networking

Industry leadership groups and communities, conferences, trade shows, corporate retreats

Community involvement and sponsorships

Figure 5-10:
Offline Marketing Communication Tools (Detailed)

Offline Channel	Marketing Application
Open House Days and Event Marketing	• Market research • Customer engagement • Reconnecting • Strengthening personal relationships • Meeting the neighbors
General networking	• Professional profile • References • Referrals
Industry leadership groups and communities, conferences, trade shows, corporate retreats	• Professional profile • References • Referrals • Education – first to know
Community involvement and sponsorships	• Brand awareness • Relationship building

5.2.1. Hosting Open House Day

The traditional Realtor technique of hosting Open House Day still has a place in the Realtor's marketing tools. However, its effectiveness may be increased by applying several creative approaches and integrating it into social-media channels and Event Marketing techniques.

Treat Open House Day as a special event; all your efforts have to be coordinated. Follow the Event Marketing Checklist (Figure 5-11) to organize yourself.

Figure 5-11:
Event Marketing Checklist

Prior to Event	Fill in Your Answer
Marketing objectives	
Guests (target audience)	

Theme	
Venue	
Date and time	
Food and beverage	
Additional services/staff	
Budget	
Invitation	
Follow-up strategy	

There are numerous opportunities to reconnect with your past clients or industry professionals. You may become known for your creative approach in Event Marketing. Don't interpret Event Marketing as strictly «party time». There are numerous ideas on planning and executing activities that will be more memorable than a traditional cocktail reception or lunch at the Brokers Open. Several creative ideas are described in Figure 5-12.

Figure 5-12:
Creative Ideas for Realtor Event Marketing

Marketing Objective	Event Approach
1. «Neighborhood Photo Shoot»: To announce that you're the Realtor in your own neighborhood.	A Realtor who is a former professional photographer sent invitations to neighbors for a professional photo shoot on the background of their own house.
2. «Santa, Help My Parents Sell the House»: To host Open House Day in the gated neighborhood where external signage is prohibited, the house is empty, and it's Christmas time.	A Realtor took a roll of paper and wrote «Santa, Help My Parents Sell the House» and attached it, hanging from the second-floor window, in front of the house. She mailed invitations to all the neighbors, and inside the empty house, she put Santa's legs hanging from the fireplace and set out cookies.

3. «First Haunted Open House Day»	A Realtor took paper skeletons and placed them in all the closets in the house. The last closet had a sign: «Stop searching for the skeletons in the closet. There are none. Buy this property». Invitations certainly had a Halloween theme.

5.2.2. General Networking

Do you know how to make connections? There are many sales coaches who teach to solely rely on cold calling as your primary technique for connecting to potential clients. I believe cold calling is purely a sales tool, not a marketing tool. Networking is a better way.

You can network anywhere – from a business after-hours event to a ball game, from the theater to a group, from a kid's party to a rock concert. Don't underestimate the power of online networking as well. And if you still think it doesn't work, you have made one of four common mistakes:

• **Mistake #1:** You choose wrong places and events at which to network.
• **Mistake #2:** You have not done your homework.
• **Mistake #3:** You did not make long-lasting first impressions.
• **Mistake #4:** You have not sealed fresh relationships by some form of follow-up.

The starting point of mastering networking is making a list of places where other people like you or people you want to meet congregate. In these places you might make a significant connection, assuming you're aware and pre-pared. Figure 5-13 helps you to come up with different networks that a Realtor can target to establish relationships within.

Figure 5-13:
Networking Checklist

Group	Existing Contacts	Need to Establish Connection with
Bankers, mortgage brokers		
Financial advisers, CPAs		
Divorce attorneys		

Immigration attorneys		
EB-5 attorneys		
Car dealers		
Insurance agents		
Florists		
General contractors		
Interior designers		
Architects		
Furniture rentals		
Stagers		
Graphic designers		
Landscapers		
Swimming pool builders		
Boat renters		

5

Helicopter, private jet services		
Professional clubs		
Local and international business referral groups		
School PTA		
Sport teams		
Funeral directors		
Other:		

Once you have selected your groups and researched their meeting formats and event calendars, choose a few venues to experience and try to consistently attend each one at least three times. After a few visits, you'll get a flavor of the value each has to you and your business. This may help you make a decision about which networks to keep on your priority list.

When you have established your priority networks, do your homework before you attend any of their meetings. Here are some tips to help you prepare for networking events:

- **Do some math.** On average, an event lasts three hours. There are two productive hours at most. On average, a conversation will last for seven to ten minutes, plus time to listen to others before your leave. You can technically make eight meaningful introductions at each event. No wonder it's so important to come prepared!
- **Know in advance who will be attending.** It's now possible to do this though different formats of invite. Do some research, and try to memorize individuals' photos. You can also invite them to connect via social media prior to an event. This is good grounds to introduce yourself face-to-face when you eventually meet.
- **Don't be afraid to get out of your comfort zone.** Remember that all people in the networking event are open and friendly for interaction. It's just a matter of being able to start interesting conversations. Simply attending the event is a waste of time. You have to do homework and the

follow-up work.

- **If you already know someone in the event, ask him or her to introduce you to people he or she already knows.** It's the easiest way to break the ice and integrate into his or her crowd.
- **«Pretend» as if you're the host of the event and greet people as if they're joining you and not vice versa.** This mind-set is a strategy to maximize results from the networking opportunities.
- **Practice your answers to the following questions.** Design and remember a memorable story about yourself. The whole personal story should not exceed one minute.
  - What do you do?
  - For whom do you do it?
  - How are you different from your peers/competitors?
- **Pay attention to details.** Be a great listener and observer.
- **Prepare a set of questions to ask your prospects, especially if you did your homework about them.** You need to know your ideal contacts for the event.
- **Practice having conversations** – paying attention, memorizing names, and repeating your own name clearly. Follow these steps to help commit others' names to memory:
  - Focus on the person.
  - Repeat his or her name aloud.
  - Ask a question.
  - Repeat the name silently.
  - Make a vivid association between the sound of the name, physical appearance, and something familiar to you.
  - Always conclude the interaction with his or her name: «It was great to meet you, Irina. I look forward to next time!»
- **Practice how to end conversations comfortably and a call for action** or some decision to move on. Take initiative to offer alternatives for further meetings, follow-up calls, or mailing additional information.
- **Dress up with some special detail that is noticeable and memorable,** and certainly follow the dress code of the occasion.
- **Take enough business cards and a pen to make notes on others' cards.** I would also recommend to take a quick immediate picture of the business card of your most important contact. Later you will save time on sorting through the stack of cards and attempting to recall the most relevant contacts. But more important than collecting business cards is establishing meaningful, memorable, and actionable conversation closings.

5.2.3. Leadership Groups and Events, Industry Leadership Groups and Communities, Conferences, Trade Shows, and Corporate Retreats

Attending conferences, industry conventions, trade shows, and corporate retreats is a special way to be around people representing the same industry/profession and see how they act. Some of the best informal networking happens during these events because the majority of people treat them as nonworking and are therefore relaxed and open to socializing. Plus, having name badges helps with introductions. Most importantly, such events have cutting-edge industry information and industry trends.

Be wise. These are the opportunities to connect, and here are the tips to do so effectively:

- **Prepare in advance by joining online communities of the future participants.** You may already make an online introduction via social network interest group, and then during the event reconnect in person.
- **Do your homework.** Make a list of top individuals and businesses that are of the most interest and value to you. Do background research on them to have an informational basis to have conversations with them. Remember, all people like compliments!
- **Think how you can be of assistance to an individual.** Don't rush to ask!
- **Systematize the way you collect and process contacts.**
- Focus on collecting contacts, not giving contacts. Have your business cards ready, but remember, unless you happen to be of value right there in the first meeting, you may not be remembered.
- **Keep in mind some basic rules of likability:** Be authentic, positive, reliable, curious about others, and a great listener. Address similarities, address familiarity, and provide value first before asking.

5.2.4. Community Involvement and Sponsorships

Community involvement can be a very effective marketing technique, especially if you're positioning yourself to a specific niche with certain needs. Your «I care» attitude can be a strong marketing message that can go viral and land a strong, trustworthy attitude from your prospects in return.

5.3. Designing a Communication Plan

Any effective marketing is based on a plan. A good plan is based on

- a communication sequence directed at your target market – a marketing campaign
- proper timing
- a justified budget

5.3.1. Planning and Executing Marketing Campaigns

The starting point for designing a marketing campaign is outlining all possible reasons/topics/messages, which are your communication touch points with your target niche, organized in a logical sequence. In this section you need to assume the role of the **Magazine Editor-in-Chief** of your target audience's favorite magazine.

This task can appear to be an enormous job; however, to simplify, there are only
- 4 seasons
- 11 federal holidays (for more information on holidays by country visit http://en.wikipedia.org/wiki/List_of_holidays_by_country)
- 12 months
- 52 weeks

In addition, add all niche-specific reasons to «talk» to your target niche.

An effective **Communication Plan** satisfies these criteria:
- Strong branding
- Consistency
- Anticipation – logical series
- Engagement – subscribers, shares, fellowship
- Call for action

If at any part of the communication process you feel that you can't handle it by yourself, consider the following:
- Automating – Devote special time for your marketing activities and complete them in advance by scheduling, then stick to the exact dates moving forward.
- Cooperating – Partner with another agent and complete a calendar and design messages together.
- Outsourcing – Outsource to a marketer to provide such service.

5.3.2. Content Calendar

For each touch point finalize headline, determine the communication channel, search keywords, communication date and budget. Try to draft your own Content Calendar by playing a role of the Editor-in-Chief of your own Publication, which is specifically designed for your target audience.

Figure 5-14:
Content Calendar

Marketing Objective	Target Audience	Headline	Subtitle/ Details	Channel	Search Keywords	Date	Budget
To Announce Rental booking season	Luxury Tenants	5 events not to be missed during winter vacation in Miami	....	Online	Miami, things to do in Miami	Aug	$0.00
To reconnect with past clients	Past clients of waterfront properties	Miami Boat Show is larger than ...	....	Offline, phone call, Email, physical meeting	Miami Boat Show	Feb	$0.00

Design (cooperate, outsource)   **Budget**   **Schedule**   **Execute**   **Analyze (RIO)**

5.3.3. Marketing Budget

You can't hope to reap the fruit without paying for seeds. There are ways to minimize your marketing budget. The biggest effect is achieved through integrated efforts resulting in synergy and timing. It's like driving on the highway; you have to maintain a certain speed on certain parts of the road.

On average, your marketing budget should be anywhere from 10 to 25 percent of projected revenue.

> *Let's do some simple math:*
> *Net Commission earned at the end of the year = $100,000*
> *10% of $100,000 = $10,000 = $833 Monthly Marketing Budget*
> *25% of $100,000 = $25,000 = $2083 Monthly Marketing Budget*

This calculation doesn't mean that these budgets must be evenly distributed throughout a year. It serves the purpose of your water source in the irrigation pipe to grow your garden. You may consider investing a larger amount into a good solid website.

Make a list of all activities that you project to undertake to boost your market presence. Estimate the budget and align your activities with the calendar.

CHAPTER 6

7th PLATFORMS

Building and
Nurturing
Your Relationship
Network

REALTOR BRANDING:
Marketing Yourself for **REAL ESTATE SUCCESS**

PLATFORMS
Building and Nurturing Your Relationship Network

The sixth P of the Branding Model – **PLATFORMS** – focuses on strengthening your brand though creating a Customer Relationship Management System (CRM) and building strong Brand Recognition.

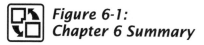
Figure 6-1:
Chapter 6 Summary

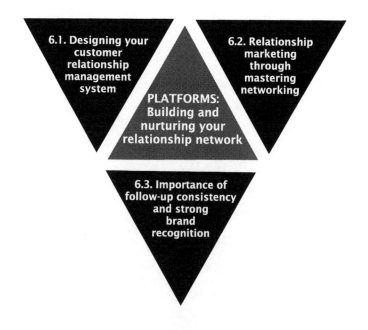

«People business» – there is no better description for real estate business. First, all of us, in some form or another, have a connection to the subject of real estate, whether being a potential buyer or seller, homeowner, tenant or landlord, real estate investor, or real estate agent. Sooner or later we all have to make decisions regarding real estate. Therefore, being an agent of choice is the ultimate goal of the real estate agent.

Assuming that after reading chapter 2 you were able to narrow down the entire pool of potential customers to a very specific market niche(s) you'll be focusing and specializing on, the message "for all your real estate needs" will no longer be featured in your marketing materials. In chapter 3 you designed your own Value Proposition and packaged it in chapter 4 to differentiate it from competitors. With achieved clarity, you're now ready to communicate your brand online and offline through numerous communication channels categorized in chapter 5. Chapter 6 will assist you in forming long-term loyal, committed relationship networks.

What exactly is a relationship network in today's real estate industry? Real estate selling and marketing components are no longer the same as what they were even five years ago. Traditional methods of sales and personal promotion are being wiped off by new technology. The Internet and globalization have redefined every aspect of marketing and sales. While you're sleeping, somebody is already browsing your website from the other side of the world. Use of videos allow customers to reduce their initial pools of property choices and not waste time driving around to look at properties in person. Real estate investors are making decisions without even physically visiting properties – with the help of publically accessible real estate resources, maps, and tools to retrieve historic data.

Realtors have realized the importance of being in tune with the markets and their customers. Embarking on investing in relationships with customers – Relationship Management – is becoming very important for the success of the real estate business. Agents are trying to identify and get to know the customer better and anticipate his or her needs for tomorrow. Especially in the recent times, where social networking is gaining ground, customer contact and relationship management is becoming more visible and instantaneous.

The main lesson to be learned is that Relationship Marketing and Network Management are the two driving forces that keep the real estate machine running full speed. Figure 6-2 summarizes this discussion.

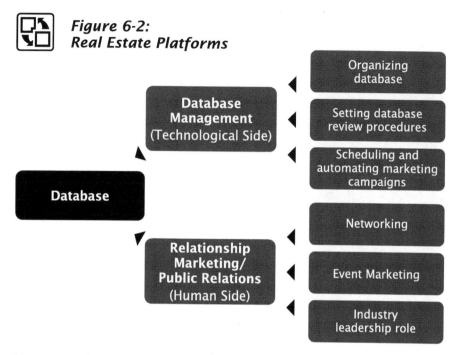

Figure 6-2:
Real Estate Platforms

Database

Database Management (Technological Side)
- Organizing database
- Setting database review procedures
- Scheduling and automating marketing campaigns

Relationship Marketing/ Public Relations (Human Side)
- Networking
- Event Marketing
- Industry leadership role

No matter where you are in your real estate career, your starting point is **database**. For the brand new agents, database is their existing contact list of their **Sphere of Influence**, the phone or e-mail contact list. For more experienced agents, this initial list has grown to include past and present clients, leads, business contacts, and more.

Following a simple rule of «Do things right the first time» will logically determine that before you run any marketing efforts in real estate, you'll organize your database. With this initial, simple effort, you're laying the fundamentals for your business. It's the technological side of your business, and if you are undecided about particular CRM application, organize your contacts in a basic Excel spreadsheet. Later, as business grows, you'll get a chance to reconsider specialized computer software or mobile applications to serve this purpose. Having a database that isn't actionable or is inconsistent won't have any positive impact on your business. Remember, it's better to have a smaller number of quality contacts than hundreds of raw data. Avoid a «junk in, junk out» situation.

Once your database takes its initial shape and form, lay down some basic habits for yourself to review the database with some regularity. Database review frequency will certainly depend on the intensity of your business, but at least once every two months is a good business procedure. It's like doing a deep cleaning of your file cabinet by going through it, removing files, relocating them, and adding notes.

When you discipline yourself to maintain your database, you'll have clarity in your marketing strategy and tactics. Therefore, a properly managed database will give you confidence to justify and pursue your marketing efforts. There is no such thing as free marketing. Even if you spend zero dollars being active online, the time you spend on networking, e-mails, and market research is marketing time and cost to you. Marketing is a business investment and, as discussed in chapter 5, anywhere from 10 to 25 percent of the expected return should be projected to be invested into the marketing of your real estate company.

Your database will become actionable once you're able to schedule and automate marketing communications, which were discussed in chapter 5. Here I'm concluding the technological side of Network Management.

The human side of your brand will only shine through human interactions. No matter how brilliant your online image is and your marketing materials are, if they aren't reinforced though your authentic brilliant personality, the brand won't even have a chance to evolve. It's the same as if you contracted a marketing agency to develop your Brand Identity and launch your brand – your legacy would finish right there and then if you didn't create a real reputation in the community you're working with and for. Therefore, in order to bring your brand to life, networking, event marketing, and strong industry leadership roles are critical aspects of building your successful real estate business.

During all these three types of activities, your level of being prepared to selectively network, effectively schedule network activities, and able to process collected contacts and take them to the next level of relationship is the key.

6.1. Designing Your Customer Relationship Management (CRM) System

In real estate, your online presence and communication consistency lay a foundation for
- lead generation
- brand awareness
- expertise

Remember, real estate is a numbers game, and the wider the funnel or the more networks you have, the more chances you have of catching a bigger fish. But in order to catch the fish, the nature of the business is such that you have to go fishing day after day.

Whether you have designed your own template or learned to use the system offered by the broker when choosing the CRM system, consider the following:

- CRM software helps you track prospects and qualifies leads and customers in an organized fashion. In addition, it may include qualifying and nourishing leads, managing marketing campaigns, building relationships, and providing service.
- It has to allow you to capture contact information, create auto responses, send properties based on clients' criteria, create mailing lists, and customize mailing campaigns and e-blasts.
- As stated before, it is important to properly establish database so that the system works for you, and not you being a slave of the system.
- Remember that 90 percent of your business is generated by following up where database becomes critical business foundation.
- Personalization must be an option; avoid turning automation into spam.
- Think about relationships in order to categorize your contacts.
- Your database must be retrievable from the CRM. In case you decide to switch the software, you must be able to export it as well as import it.

At any point of your real estate journey, being organized is critical. As time goes by, your initial database will need cleaning and regrouping. Like any process of organization, start with a simple recording system – for example, an Excel spreadsheet – then transition to a more sophisticated database system as your golden eggs start to multiply. Initial setup and consistent maintenance are the keys to managing your business in the long run because, by the end of the day, it's all about managing and communicating to your client database.

Discipline yourself. This is one top habit that any Realtor should develop and stick to. Prove to yourself that you're not like many real estate professionals, where part of your database is on a spreadsheet on your computer and another part is in your phone address book. And there are probably some names and phone numbers on napkins, business cards, and scraps of paper on or around your desk, in the glove box of your car, in your day planner, and balled up in your briefcase or purse. If there's no rhyme or reason to the order, like a raffle, you will only contact whomever you happened to stumble upon while cleaning out your personal belongings.

It's time to get organized! Without an organized database, with your clients' information located in one place, you may spend most of your day trying to market your services to the wrong people. Creating your database is a vital part of developing a system that will generate a predictable stream of referred leads.

Your database is more than a list of contact information; it's a list of relationships. It allows you to focus your lead generation activities and marketing budget. When you sort and qualify your database, you can focus your attention on the clients who will be an integral part of your success by sending referrals to you. As a result of the attention and value you provide, these clients are more likely to tell their friends, families, and neighbors about the great services you offer and send referrals your way. Marketing to people you already know allows you to build upon the existing relationships that generate referrals. This is done through personal note cards, phone calls, client lunches, and so on, using an effective real estate CRM.

Properly set priority target markets allow you to prioritize your activities and marketing budget. There are many ways to sort your database. Below is one example.

Graded Contacts: Regardless of the size of your database, and whether you have an existing database or are starting from scratch and making a list of everyone you know, you can simply start with the following categories:
- **A+** clients are people who have sent you multiple referrals.
- **A** clients are people who are most likely to refer you.
- **B** clients are people who would refer you, if asked and shown how.
- **C** clients are people who might refer you in the future.
- **D** clients are people to be deleted from your database.

It's important to give attention to your entire database, except for those D clients who should be deleted. Your A+ and A clients should receive the most attention, receiving phone calls, personal note cards, or invitations to client parties. Once you've taken care of these clients, shift your focus to your B clients, and then to your C clients.

The sorting process should be repeated every few months, especially if you're frequently adding new people to your database, for example, when referrals are sent your way. Don't worry; it may seem like a tedious process now, but once you have all of your contacts in one place, instead of located in various places around your home and office, it will take just a few minutes of your time.

Relationship Contacts: Another alternative to grouping your contacts is based on the type of the relationship you have with each of them. Your communication style and approach truly is based on how close your relationships are with particular people. For example, your categories could be «friends and family,» «colleagues,» and «partners.» Overall, all potential clients can be divided into three categories, as illustrated in Figure 6-3.

Figure 6-3:
Client Types

Categories	Subcategories
People You Know – Gold Database	• Present clients • Past clients • Sphere of influence (family, friends, colleagues within industry, strategic partners outside industry, former colleagues)
People Who Visited Your Store – Window Shoppers	• Clients you have interacted with, have not purchased yet
People You Don't Know – Cold Leads	• Website traffic • Social-media followers, subscribers • Direct marketing leads

6.2. Relationship Marketing through Mastering Networking

The golden rule of any networking is "Give more than you get." If you reset your mind by focusing on selection of the interest groups in which you're truly committed to participate and contribute to, this strategy will take you a long way and pay substantial dividends. A person who has mastered networking is the one who

- leads or at least participates in networking consistently;
- volunteers/contributes his or her time and effort for a common goal;
- takes responsibility in the activities;
- inspires and helps others;
- genuinely expresses an interest in other people;
- shares information; and
- sincerely introduces people to one another.

The good news is that in order to build your network of potential connections, which can generate business, you don't have to start from zero. At some point in time most people will have a need for real estate service. Each of us has a circle of friends, it's your initial target audience, and most of the time, once the sphere expands, it does primarily become your Class A and A+ Clients.

You have to be strategic with your networking effort because it's all about effectiveness in time spent. Don't rely strictly on luck to meet somebody.

The easiest way to increase your network is to identify groups and communities in which you can share the same interests, such as:

- professional meetings
- clubs
- related industry meetings and events
- social groups
- classes to learn new hobbies
- fitness classes
- school volunteer groups
- sport activities and practices
- gardening clubs

6.3. Importance of Follow-up Consistency and Strong Brand Recognition

Use a follow-up schedule. Don't leave follow-up to chance. Most brokers fail to invest in setting and communicating clear expectations for what good follow-up actually looks like beyond some vague generalities. Get specific. Create a follow-up schedule that outlines when calls and e-mail follow-ups should be happening.

Starting out, two basic contact schedules should suffice, one for active leads and another for passive leads. Active leads are responsive and ready to buy or sell in the near term. Passive leads are still qualified but are on a long-term buying timeframe. Follow-up schedules can and should extend all the way out to twelve months, although the tone and frequency of communications should change significantly as time goes on, based on the level of interest displayed from the prospect.

Follow this algorithm to connect:

- Collect a card.
- E-mail personal messages to connect. It could be an e-mail in which you refresh the contact and e-mail all necessary links if, for example, you want people to subscribe to your blog.
- Friend/connect with the new contact through all primary social-media channels.
- Don't think that you have to meet with everyone in person. Make decisions depending on potential, time, and effort. Assign a category to the contact to direct that contact to a certain part in your database. Be a master organizer of your Contact Management System.

By mastering traditional networking and taking it to another level, you have great chances to excel in your authentic marketing efforts.

7 CHAPTER

PROJECTION

Pursuing the Future with Persistence

7 PROJECTION
Pursuing the Future
with Persistence

The seventh P of the Branding Model – **PROJECTION** – is focused on growing your brand.

 Figure 7-1:
Chapter 7 Summary

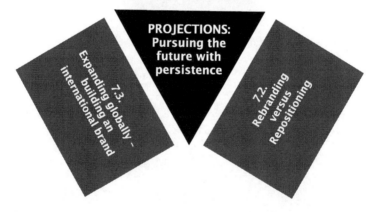

Congratulations! You have now completed the journey of designing and moving forward with your personal brand. I assume you have done a great job and you're proud of the Personal Brand that is your full representation.

However, treat this accomplishment as the beginning, not the end. As you're changing and gaining more experience, your personal brand also evolves.

Additionally, your personal brand exists in a business environment that isn't static. Taking these two facts into account, your Personal Branding helps you avoid the need to continually reinvent yourself. Instead, you're taking a new role, the role of the Brand Manager with a wide scope of responsibilities. You're never «done» with the subject of Personal Branding. In fact, if you ignore your brand, you'll fall into the trap of being «like everyone else» and become a commodity again.

7.1.   Grow Your Brand through Brand Management

Brand Management is the process of maintaining, improving, and leveraging a brand so that the name is associated with positive results. Brand management is built on a marketing foundation, but it focuses directly on the brand and how that brand can remain favorable to customers while differentiating from competition.

Personal Brand Management involves a number of important aspects:
* **Authenticity** – Your personal brand must show the real you at all times, not a fake version of you. You're the foundation of your legacy and authentic reputation.
* **Focus** – To break through, you have to focus on the market niche.
* **Value** – Your value proposition differentiates you from your competition.
* **Innovation** – Innovate to stay current. Invest in yourself.
* **Customer Service** – This is your moment of truth; great performances generate memories.
* **Communication Consistency** – The synergy effect may only be reached through consistency.
* **Branding** – Stay loyal to your signature look.
* **Cost** – Track your marketing expenses.

7.2.   Rebranding versus Repositioning

In the situation that your brand is no longer relevant, or you want to totally rethink and redesign, you have two options:
* **Rebrand**
* **Reposition your brand**

When you **rebrand**, you change the entire image of your brand. The rebranding decision can be relevant in the situation, for example, when you decide to establish a brand based on a fictitious name or personal name and no longer use the broker's brand as your brand name.

Rebranding typically includes changing most or all of your Brand Identity elements, such as the name, icon, colors, type font, and tagline. The identity change may also be accompanied by brand repositioning.

However, a brand can be repositioned without changing its identity – for example, when you decide to upgrade your target niche, especially if your new target market is more upscale than the one you have already established presence and reputation with.

Repositioning focuses on changing what customers associate with the brand and sometimes competing brands. This usually entails a change in the brand's promise and its personality. Taglines often change with brand repositioning in order to communicate the new promise. And sometimes the identity itself is updated or refreshed to reinforce the change in the brand's positioning. Most brand repositioning projects don't result in completely changed identities. Usually the brand name doesn't change, and frequently, neither do the identity elements, other than the tagline and perhaps a slight update to the identity system.

Another way to understand the rebranding and repositioning processes is to visualize the brand as a person. If a person rebrands him- or herself, he or she may gain or lose weight, change the style and color of his or her hair, get a new wardrobe, and perhaps change his or her name. If the person repositions him- or herself, he or she changes his or her values, attitude, personality, or behavior. Any combination of these changes can occur together or separately.

In summary, rebranding is an identity change. Repositioning is a change in the brand's promise, personality, or other associations. These changes can be performed together or separately. In other words, it is repeating Personal Branding Cycle again.

Here are a few things to consider when you prepare for necessary changes:

- Don't use age as an excuse to not use cutting-edge technology. Remember, you're a lifelong learner. **Update your skills.** Remember that new technology is supposed to make life easier, not harder.
- Focus on what you have gained from your **previous work experience** that no younger person has to offer.
- **Start with a narrowly defined niche,** such as a community or particular buildings.
- Are your **appearance and image current?**
- **Connect with industry and nonindustry (local) groups and associations.**
- **Craft and update all your profiles.**
- **Reconnect and build your network, thereby updating your database.**
- **Seek out volunteer opportunities** that will allow you to expand your network, get on-the-job training, and be exposed to market knowledge.
- **Stay enthusiastic, positive, and inspired** to wonder and question the process. Don't be frustrated if you don't meet people who are open to sharing immediately. There are always plenty of training opportunities to

address all your questions.

- **Don't be afraid to learn new things.** If you're not an active user of social media, watch how-to videos or read a book about it – or ask a teenager.
- **Avoid perfectionism.** It will slow you down. No one is great at the beginning. Just start, and you'll build your ways. It's likely that not all tools and media channels will be your favorites, but you need to understand them all and then stick to a few.
- **Plan your time and marketing budget.** Set marketing goals. Prospecting and learning are key at the beginning.
- **Substitute frustration with a good sense of humor.**
- **Keep in mind your core values and stick to them.** It's obvious that during transition, it's always easy to lose the core.
- **Be proactive. Try new ideas.**

7.3. Expanding Globally – Building an International Brand

Your personal brand isn't universal due to cultural differences that you have to be aware of.

Your Personal Brand Formula is determined by your target market; therefore, if the clients have changed, your task is to adjust your brand to the cultural insights of your potential new clientele.

These are the questions to be addressed:
- Do your brand characteristics have the same interpretation when used internationally as in your home market? Does the new target audience value them as much as your home clients?
- How do you communicate differently to your international clients? Which channels will be priority channels?
- How much and which aspects do you need to modify of the American version of your brand?
- What are the don'ts to be aware of when dealing with specific cultures? Study business etiquette.
- What are the visible components to focus attention on or to omit?
- What are the economic, political, social, and technological trends in the country you're expanding your business to?

CONCLUSION

Congratulations, my fellow Realtors, on following through with the 7 Ps Personal Branding Model!

If you have successfully completed all the exercises as recommended, you're now the owner of your defined personal brand, a brand that you can be sure and proud of. From now on, everything you do is building, promoting, and enhancing your personal brand and knowing the difference.

No matter where you are in your real estate career, this book will always provide you with marketing and branding blueprint in order to take charge of real estate opportunities and momentum.

ACKNOWLEDGMENTS

This book is dedicated to my father, Alexey Kim, and mother, Lyubov Kim, for their infinite patience and support for all my projects; to my dearest husband, Michael Sang, for his belief in my reaching heights I only dream of and the freedom to soar; and to my son, Alexandr Kim, for his tolerance and independence.

I would like to thank and recognize the following people:

- Jill Hertzberg and Jill Eber – «the Jills» – the number-one team worldwide among eighty-five thousand Coldwell Banker real estate professionals, whom I had the privilege of working for briefly as a marketing manager before transitioning to full-time Realtor. They have inspired me.
- Nancy Klock Corey, manager of the Coldwell Banker Miami Beach Office, for her guidance and personal undivided attention.
- The Miami Association of Realtors Leadership Board and staff for raising industry standards through education and Realtor support.

ABOUT the AUTHOR

Born in Almaty, Kazakhstan, and educated in the United States and Europe, Irina brings her passion for marketing and international business experience to the Elite Club of the Coldwell Banker Previews Agents, whose marketing expertise has been proved by multimillion-dollar transactions in 2014. Successful performance within just two and a half years as a Realtor resulted in Irina earning the Coldwell Banker International President's Elite 2014 Award and the Florida Top 100 2014 Award.

Having two master's degrees – an MBA from the University of Colorado and an MPhil in marketing from the Maastricht School of Management, Netherlands – and being a professional marketer with fourteen years of corporate marketing experience in such brands as Pizza Hut and KFC among countries like Russia, Kazakhstan, and the United Arab Emirates, Irina has made successful transition to the real estate industry within the leading Coldwell Banker Brand, a logical career step with her relocation to Miami in 2010. Irina engaged in lecturing for a wide spectrum of marketing courses at universities in Kazakhstan and the Czech Republic from 2000 to 2009.

Irina is currently developing the www.MiamiForRussian.com/ www.MiamiForRussian.ru brand, the website specifically addressing all real estate issues for Russian-speaking clients looking to invest, live in, and enjoy Miami and South Florida. The website features highly advanced tools that allow the clients to get familiar not only with properties but also with neighborhoods through the use of floor plans, videos, interactive maps, virtual tours, aerial views, and so forth.

Irina is an active member of the Miami Association of Realtors, contributing to the development of real estate trainings, and was awarded Innovation in Education Award 2015. She serves on the Young Professionals Network Leadership Board.

Irina is positioning her personal brand as Marketing Strategist, Author and Educator. She is also entrepreneur and partner in several businesses in which she performs major strategic visionary and marketing role (IrinaKimSang.com, MiamiVerticalGarden.com).

LIST OF EXHIBITS

7 Ps PERSONAL BRANDING MODEL

CHAPTER 1
PRODUCT: Knowing Yourself

CHAPTER 2
PEOPLE AND PLACE: Knowing Your Niche

3 CHAPTER 3
POSITIONING: Aligning Yourself with Your Niche

4 CHAPTER 4
PACKAGING: Designing Brand Identity

5P CHAPTER 5
PROMOTION: Communicating Your Brand
Online and Offline

6P CHAPTER 6
PLATFORMS: Building and Nurturing Your
Relationship Network

7P CHAPTER 7
PROJECTION: Pursuing the Future with Persistence

Made in the USA
Charleston, SC
28 May 2016